How to Save $100,000 a Year on Google AdWords

TRAFFIC DOMINATION - How To Use A Blog Network To Dominate Your Niche, Generate Leads For Free, And Save $100,000 A Year In Google AdWords Advertising Costs

Jeremy Taylor

Published by
Inspired Publishing Books
Inspired Publishing Ltd
27 Old Gloucester Street
London
WC1N 3AX

TABLE OF CONTENTS

PREFACE

This book was written by Internet Marketing Expert Jeremy Taylor who has made a significant investment in time and money trialling different internet marketing strategies and products to understand not only what works, but why it works.

The result is a new strategy in internet marketing called the "Social Blog Network", a hybrid strategy of other proven techniques that are being used today, and it can help you to generate the equivalent amount of business as spending $100,000 on Google AdWords.

In this book, you will find a step-by-step guide on how to create your own Social Blog Network—enabling you to significantly increase your online presence, generate tons of free traffic, reduce your dependency on paid search, reduce your costs, and ultimately—improve your profits.

NB. The internet is constantly evolving so if you wish to be informed of the latest developments and related news please take time to subscribe to the email newsletter at www.socialblog.network/newsletter

INTRODUCTION

If you have picked up this book because of its intriguing title, then like me, you have probably spent a lot of time and money trying to get your head around the complexities of Google AdWords and other online advertising platforms with varying levels of success. This book, despite its name, is not about how to make better use of those platforms— there are already plenty of courses, tips, and videos online that will teach you how to do that. What it will teach you is how to maximise your online presence for little cost and reduce your reliance on **paid search**.

I've tried to keep the tone of the book at a non-technical level, however we are talking about marketing on the internet, so I apologise in advance if you feel that we're getting a little deep at times. That said, ten years ago creating a website would have required technical knowledge, but fortunately these days, there are content management systems available to take care of all of that for you.

When I left school back in the eighties, the internet didn't exist and personal computing was a relatively new field.

Luckily, our school was one of the first to teach computing and I quickly realised that I had an affinity for it, so it wasn't long before I made IT my profession. Now, some thirty years later, I've worked in all sorts of businesses, from small IT consultancies through to huge blue chip companies, much of which was in the development and support of software across all types of business, including sales and marketing. During that time, I've seen from the beginning how the internet has changed our lives, and especially how to market and sell online.

To get to the top of the search engines in the early days, you could get a long way by registering a domain name that contained your search keywords and then stuffing your page title, **metatags**, and page content with the same keywords. However, that technique didn't last long, as search engines became more sophisticated. Google in particular has a reputation for redesigning their ranking algorithms—the things that determine which sites get listed first. You may have heard of a couple of famous algorithm changes that Google released codenamed "Panda" and "Penguin", which were notorious for radically changing the way their search engine ranked websites for keywords—and put many websites out of business overnight in the process.

With Google being the most popular search engine on the planet, the Panda change in 2011 and Penguin in 2013 caused shockwaves among the marketing community and led many marketers to do exactly what Google wanted and drop search engine optimisation methods (**SEO** for short) in favour of the more expensive but reliable paid search.

In the years that followed, SEO techniques have continued to be developed, but due to the fear brought about by Panda and Penguin, they are often ignored by many companies, who see them as unreliable options.

This mentality is one of the reasons why online advertising has become such a huge industry, with companies such as Google (Alphabet Inc.), Facebook, Yahoo, and so on enjoying meteoric success, and literally generating billions of dollars in revenue from businesses around the globe. Google in particular has been very inventive with their products in an attempt to match advertisers directly with consumers, and both Google and Facebook have continued to report a steady increase in revenue every quarter. Just take a look at the figures...

Company	Gross Revenue (millions)	Net Income after Tax (millions)	3 Month Accounting Period Ending
Google	$ 22,451	$5,061	Sept 2016
Facebook	$ 6,436	$2,055	June 2016
Yahoo	$ 1,035	$47	Sept 2016

With inventiveness comes complexity, and with so many ways you can advertise, Google has created a training course backed up with an "AdWords Certification" accreditation program. This course covers modules such as AdWords Fundamentals, Search, Display, Mobile, Video, and Shopping adverts to ensure all the available options are fully understood.

The **Google** AdWords **certification** is a professional accreditation that **Google** offers to individuals who demonstrate proficiency in basic and advanced aspects of AdWords. An AdWords **certification** allows individuals to demonstrate that **Google** recognises them as an expert in online advertising.

About the AdWords certification - Google Partners Help
https://support.**google**.com/partners/answer/3154326?hl=en-GB

Facebook also has an eLearning and Certification program, and given the costs involved in advertising on either Facebook or Google, it makes sense to complete the training before spending a cent—or you will be flushing your marketing budget down the drain.

Having worked for many years as an Internet Marketing Consultant, I have witnessed the shift in direction unfold to paid search—and I felt it was time that I do something to help more businesses take advantage of natural search traffic.

I should point out that I have nothing against paid search; in fact, I highly recommend it for companies who are breaking into a new market as it allows them to test new campaigns without doing too much work. However, what many businesses fail to do once they have proved that a paid campaign works is to look at ways of bringing down the cost. Surely at this point it would make sense to explore other, less expensive methods of achieving the same results. Additionally, any marketing professional will tell you that a good marketing strategy has as many ways to generate interest from potential customers as possible— that way, should one fail, you will always have another source to take its place.

Now, the interesting dichotomy that search engines face is that the information they hold is what attracts users to their service—information that whilst useful, does not necessarily result in a business case that justifies paying for adverts. Search engines therefore have to provide results in the form of free listings as well as paid advertising to be able to justify their existence. After all, the reason we use them is because of the huge amount of information they hold.

Google, in fact, goes out of its way to provide lots of tools and information on how to maximise the listing for your website in their directory. They have even published a series of guidelines on how to ensure your site is listed on their search engine, all of which are freely available to website owners, and are summarized here:

- Make pages primarily for users, not for search engines.
- Don't deceive your users, and avoid tricks intended to improve search engine rankings.

- Think about what makes your website unique, valuable, or engaging. Make your website stand out from others in your field.

Google provides this advice because they want users of their products to have the best possible experience and are more than happy to help website owners with that goal.

In short, Google is willing to help you optimise your pages in their search engine however you need to focus on providing good content that people will want to read—Google will respect that and in return, will list your web pages ranked in relation to others. However, just doing what Google asks doesn't guarantee much, so I'll provide my own recommendations for you in the next chapter.

CHAPTER 1

How to Market Yourself on the Internet

There is a lot of psychology that goes into Sales and Marketing, so before we get into the details of how to market yourself on the internet, there are a few fundamentals you need to understand first—and where better to learn this than from the professionals?

One of the first IT jobs I had in my youth was working in the sales administration office of a Timeshare company in the Spanish Canary Islands off the coast of Morocco. The islands are incredibly popular with European tourists due to the good all year-round weather and so are an ideal place to set up a holiday business.

Timeshare was a relatively new concept at the time, although one with an increasingly bad reputation due to the high-pressure sales methods they employed. However, I found the work interesting, the lifestyle was fun, and without realising it, over the next four years I learned a huge amount about marketing and selling, which is still relevant today.

Interestingly, the way the sales process worked was for a salesman to take couples for a tour around the resort, during which time they chatted about holidays and built up a relationship with them. At the end of the tour, the couple would be taken to a sales area via a wall full of Polaroid photographs of couples who had already bought timeshares (remember this idea—it's called **social proof**). The salesperson would then sit the couple down at a table among other couples and pitch them an offer that was so good, it was difficult to say no. Naturally, the price would start high and if they bought today, they were entitled to a big discount (encouragement to sign *on the day*).

During the conversation, the salesman would get the couple to focus on their ideal apartment and week, which introduced scarcity into the equation, putting more pressure on them to sign on the day. Then as people bought, out came the champagne and corks would pop around the sales floor, providing more social proof. Humans are often referred to as "sheep" as we are so easily influenced by the decisions of others, and with champagne corks popping across the room, it was like lambs to the slaughter.

Warming up a Cold Lead

If you analyse this process, you can see that the sales company fully understood the principle that "people do business with people they know, like, and trust". This phrase, incidentally, was coined by Dale Carnegie back in 1936—the author of the famous book "How to Win Friends and Influence People".

Couples touring the resort were often referred to as "cold leads" within the sales department and the tour gave the salespeople an opportunity to build a relationship with the couple, known as "the warm up", before pitching the product.

If you think about it, any visitor coming to your website for the first time is a cold lead, and cold leads rarely buy because they don't trust you—so you have to warm them up first and earn that trust. With online selling, you don't have the customer sitting in front of you, however you can build trust *virtually* using the following methods:

- Create a warm and inviting online experience.

- Publish relevant stories online via a blog and social media.

- Build an email mailing list that engages potential clients over time by delivering relevant information.

- Build up a following on social media with regular updates.

Each one of these methods is covered in this book.

Social Proof

Remember the Polaroids of the happy customers—social proof is a very important part of the sales process, as no one wants to be the first to buy something that is untested. You need to provide evidence that you're a reliable company who everyone loves doing business with, and the easiest way to do this is by publishing customer testimonials.

Testimonials need to be convincing, so I wouldn't recommend simply adding a few lines of static text on your website. Ideally, they need to come from an independent source, and there are many companies out there who provide this service. I'll touch on a few of these in chapter 8, which discusses Reputation Marketing.

You can also use your blog to build up social proof, but it needs to be a convincing story with photographs that provide evidence that the job was done well. If you can get a photo of the customer on there, then even better. In fact, with the ability to shoot short videos on smartphones these days, you could even make a video testimonial, but make it convincing by adding detail into the script.

Building an online following via social media also provides great social proof, as potential customers are far more likely to trust a company with 3,000 Facebook likes or 10,000 Twitter followers.

Recommendations are another great way to build social proof, as it's well evidenced that you are far more likely to get a sale from someone as a result of a recommendation than from a cold lead visiting your site for the first time.

Content is King

Back in 1996, Bill Gates published an article on the future of the internet where he coined the phrase "Content is King", and he foretold that there was money to be made by publishing content.

"Content is where I expect much of the real money will be made on the Internet, just as it was in broadcasting.

The television revolution that began half a century ago spawned a number of industries, including the manufacturing of TV sets, but the long-term winners were those who used the medium to deliver information and entertainment."

Bill Gates 1/3/1996

The internet was only just getting going back then, so it was quite a bold statement. Looking back, you can see that he was absolutely right.

It's clear that if you want to get noticed on the internet, you need to do what Bill suggested and start producing content. In fact, there are trillions of web pages in the Google Index, which is a huge amount of content. It's a simple mathematical deduction, therefore, that the more references you have in that index, the bigger your exposure and chance of discovery.

The Google Search Algorithm

The main reason that Google is the most popular search engine in the world today is down to the quality of its search experience. With trillions of web pages to analyse, Google has managed to work out an efficient method of categorising each one and ranking it in order of popularity and relevance.

The exact algorithm that search engines use to decide which websites are more important than others is a well-kept secret, however it's worth remembering that search engines are simply huge banks of computers processing large volumes of text, and by tweaking that text and other factors, we can improve the ranking of our sites.

One thing we do know about the algorithm is that it takes into account over 100 different signals, which can broadly be divided into four main groups: Keywords, Links, Domain, and Environment. The following infographic should give you a taste of the complexity involved.

Domain Registration

One of the factors that Google considers is the domain name, so it's important to get it right from the outset. At the time of writing, there are over 800 **TLDs** (Top Level Domain Extensions) available to choose from, including the original .com, .org, .mil, and .edu through to Geographic and Category TLDs. This is about to change, however, as ICANN—the organisation who manages TLDs—have big plans to release hundreds more TLDs that will take the choice to over 1,000.

For a full list of TLDs, take a look at the following web page, which lists them all chronologically from 1985.

http://blog.europeandomaincentre.com/list-of-domain-extensions/

These new TLDs will certainly have an impact in the future, but for the time being, you have the following groups to choose from:

- Geographic
- Generic
- Business
- Commerce
- Education
- Finance
- Food & Drink
- Government
- Industry
- Lifestyle & Personal
- Media
- Professional
- Real Estate
- Sport
- Technology
- Travel

Google likes to categorise domains, so it makes sense to choose an extension that will encourage Google to rank it for that category. For example, if your site relates to travel, choose a Travel domain such as .cruises, .flights, or .rentals. Alternatively, to target a particular region, choose a geographic domain e.g. .co.uk, .london, .eu, .tokyo, or .vegas. If none of that makes sense, you can't go wrong by registering a .com, as it is fairly generic and is the most well-known of all the TLDs.

Once you have chosen your TLD, then you can give thought to the domain name itself, which ideally will be based around a keyword that is highly relevant to the niche the website it relates to.

 Use a keyword, or keywords, in your domain name and make it as short and memorable as possible.

There are a number of factors to take into account when choosing a domain, including:

Age – The longer a domain has existed in the Google Index, the more trust and authority it will have created.

Expiry – Long expiry dates are a good indication of maturity; it also works out to be more cost-effective.

WhoIs – Register the domain in the country you are targeting and avoid using the privacy feature, which implies you are hiding something.

15

Although getting the right domain name gives you a good foundation, the most important elements of ranking in the Google index are the keywords you use in your website content and links from external websites.

Content and Keywords

There is a whole chapter dedicated to the importance of choosing the right keywords later in this book; however, for the purposes of the Google index, it's important to understand that you will only rank for keywords if they are included in the content, title, and headings of a page. This statement also applies to media included in the page, such as the name and titles of images and videos. Don't overdo it though, as Google employs a ratio of keyword use and other words to calculate keyword density, and a page can be ranked down because of it, so aim for a density between 0.5 and 2.5% to be safe.

Links

It may sound old-fashioned, but the fact is, the way Google ranks a site for importance is actually based on a principle of recommendations. Naturally, it's more complex than that, but essentially, Google is constantly scanning the internet to see how websites link to each other—and it sees links as recommendations. Those sites with the most links pointing to them are ranked in the index as the most popular and therefore are shown higher up in the search listings.

All of this sounds simple, but the fact is, Google's search ranking algorithm is very complex and uses a large number of factors to decide how to rank pages for search keywords. However, it's well-known that it the algorithm is greatly influenced by the links that point to a web page.

Of course, the number of links is one factor, but to rank highly for the right keyword, you need to ensure that the text *within* the link that points to your page (known as the **anchor text**) uses text that matches the keywords you wish the page to rank for. So, say you want your website to rank for the term "Weight Loss Expert", it would undoubtedly help if numerous other sites had links to your website with the anchor text "Weight Loss Expert", e.g.:

<a href="http://www.mysite.com">Weight Loss Expert</a>

If you're a non-technical person, this is the mark-up code used in a web page to link to another site. This code is usually referred to as **HTML**, or Hyper Text Mark-up Language, and is interpreted by web browsers to look like the following:

Weight Loss Expert

One popular way of visualising how Google works is to count these links as votes—the more votes you have, the higher up the rankings for a search term you are likely to rise.

Another factor to consider is the importance of the page linking to you, which is often called its level of **authority**, and the page's relevance to your niche. So, if a website linking to your website is seen by Google as an **authority** for a particular keyword, then some of that authority will "rub off" on your site, which in turn helps your site rank. The same goes for relevance, so for maximum effect, you want to get **backlinks** from other sites in the same niche. You often hear this referred to as **link juice**, and the more important and relevant the site linking to your page, the stronger the juice.

Environment

In 2016, the Google Chrome web browser was updated to warn users about sites that allow you to log on, but have not implemented encryption.

This is an indication of how important Google sees encryption, and has publicly stated that it uses this as another signal in its ranking algorithm. Installing encryption on your own site will depend on your hosting company, so talk to them about purchasing and installing an **SSL** certificate.

On the subject of hosting, it makes sense to choose a company based in the country you're targeting due to the very nature of the speed of light, as it will offer a quicker response. Another factor to consider is the speed of the server itself, as most low-cost hosting is provided on shared servers, which may actually host hundreds of other sites. This will result in a slower response compared to a dedicated server. Google is known to use response times as a factor in its algorithm, so it's worth keeping a watch on how the server is performing and move the site to another hosting company if required.

Summary

Here's a quick recap of the most important points in this chapter:

- Research **all** the relevant search keywords for your niche.
- Choose the right domain name from the outset.
- Build an engaging and informative website that allows you to publish stories about your business based around relevant search keywords.
- Capture and publish customer success stories.
- Use social media to build up a following and reputation.
- Get relevant links from **authority sites**.
- Start a mailing list to warm up your potential clients with stories and information about your business.

Don't be overwhelmed by this list, as the following chapter outlines a successful strategy to follow, and you'll see that with the right tools and guidance, it takes a lot less work to implement than you might think.

CHAPTER 2

The Social Blog Network Strategy

So, how do we publish lots of content and generate plenty of links to give that content a push within Google? Well, the easiest way is via a WordPress blog, which for the un-initiated is basically a piece of software that doesn't require any technical knowledge such as HTML, and allows you to easily manage your online presence. Many businesses already have this in place, but very few use it to its full potential.

There is, of course, more to it than just setting up a blog for your company, so to give you a taste, I've put together the following list of steps. These are the exact steps I follow when setting up a new blog and we'll go into these in more detail in the following chapters.

1) Research your niche to understand which keywords to target.

2) Set up your WordPress site with the appropriate theme.

3) Create social media accounts on all platforms.

4) Set up WordPress plugins to automate posting to social media.

5) Register your site with Google's and Bing's Webmaster tools.

6) Register your site with reputation services to build social proof.

7) Create and publish content around your keywords.

These are the minimum steps that should be completed when setting up any blog. While this process may sound simple, what you are left with is an almost-perfect content publishing system that—combined with social media— ensures every post gets picked up by Google and has links pointing to it.

There is one flaw with this approach though, as the number of links you can get back from your own social media posts will be limited, so to really get the link juice flowing, you need to find ways to get more links—ideally from authority sites in your niche. Achieving this is not that simple, as most un-solicited requests for links tend to be ignored. But have no fear, there is a solution!

Let's take this idea one step further and imagine you have multiple blogs, all of which were configured using the process just described, with each post cross-referencing other blogs and social media to build a huge network of links. What you will have created is a very powerful socially connected publishing platform that we call a **Social Blog Network** or **SBN**.

Social Blog Network

By definition, a blog network is a large number of blogging sites under your direct control containing posts that cross-link to each other, and in turn link to your primary website site, often referred to as "the money site".

The simplest way to understand this is shown in the following diagram, where each circle is a website; the outer sites in link to the middle sites which in turn link to the primary site shown in the centre of the diagram in blue.

This is also magnified by the links coming in from the posts on the social media accounts connected to each site. The result is a great deal of link juice being generated, all of which is targeted at the primary site, so it ends up ranking higher.

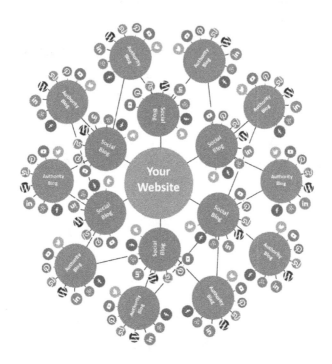

To explain this, we'll look at a real-life example...

Some years back, I started working with a small firm called Tile Doctor Ltd near Lancaster in the north west of England. They are experts in the tile, stone, and grout cleaning niche, which has become increasingly popular over the last ten years. The company have numerous related products and services available and wanted to increase their online exposure in order to grow their business.

Like most companies, they had heard a lot of talk about how SEO didn't work, how the **Google algorithm** was impossible to crack, and how AdWords was the only reliable way to get to the top of the search listings. However, the tile and stone market was really taking off in the UK, competition was increasing, and they couldn't afford to launch an expensive AdWords-based marketing campaign that would have resulted in a bidding war with their competition. Advertisers just love it when competitors go head to head like this, as in reality, they are the only party who can win in the end.

Tile Doctor wanted to attract customers to its local tile cleaning service as well as selling the large range of products at a national level, all of which resulted in a very long list of relevant keywords.

Still a believer in SEO, my recommendation was to overpower the competition by flooding the search engines with as much information about Tile Doctor as possible, and to take advantage of the fact that search engines still needed to provide users with a good search experience. I was already aware of the simplicity and power of the WordPress blogging software after implementing several installations for other customers, and I realised it would make a perfect platform for the campaign. On top of that, Google had started introducing local search into its results in order to provide users with more relevant results, so I planned to implement the sites to take maximum advantage of that as well.

With an increasing army of Tile Doctors around the UK providing stories of their activities, it was just a question of setting up the blogs (around 10 initially) and posting their stories.

The stories we posted would not only provide search engines with content for its index, they would also serve a second purpose—building trust and creating an initial relationship with potential customers, who after reading the blogs would be left in little doubt that Tile Doctor was an expert in their field.

As we've discussed, links are an important part of the Google algorithm, so to make this campaign as successful as possible, we also needed to generate relevant backlinks to the stories being posted. So, we set up more WordPress blogs and social media accounts to provide this.

Think of each Tile Doctor blog as the middle "Social Blog" circles in the SBN diagram. Each post that detailed a job they completed also included backlinks to the products they used on the main Tile Doctor website, which is represented by the "Your Website" circle in the centre of the diagram.

Today, the Tile Doctor blogs have over 1,500 posts, each one of which points back to the products on the Tile Doctor website. That's a lot of link juice! This is then compounded as the posts are **syndicated** to social media accounts on Google+, Twitter, Facebook, etc.

Another advantage of this strategy is that the outer series of websites in the SBN diagram become authority sites as they hold details of activities relating to one subject matter.

A good example of an Authority site is http://limestone.tilecleaning.co.uk, which at the time of writing contains 86 posts all relating to the maintenance and cleaning of limestone tiles. Each of the posts is syndicated to its own set of social media accounts and links back to the original post on the Tile Doctor blog with anchor text such as "Limestone Cleaning Expert in Suffolk", as well as other relevant sites.

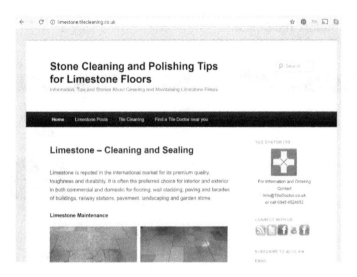

There are many authority-type sites in the Tile Doctor SBN—
one for every type of tile and situation you can imagine,
including the following examples:

- http://church-floor.tilecleaning.co.uk,

- http://fireplace.tilecleaning.co.uk,

- http://pamment.tilecleaning.co.uk

- http://worktop.tilecleaning.co.uk

All of these sites are owned and controlled by Tile Doctor
and form the basis of their SBN.

It's an effective strategy that works very well in the UK due
to the use of the geographical .co.uk TLD. For example,
searching on Google with the phrase "Limestone Tile
Cleaning" shows that Google now considers the

Limestone.TileCleaning.co.uk site as an authority on the subject—ranking it in third position. Interestingly, the Tile Doctor Limestone page is ranked in first place due to all the link juice it has received from the network.

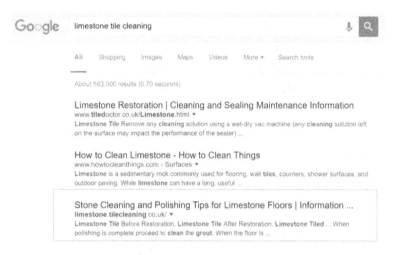

Naturally, as I mentioned earlier, these websites did not come into existence overnight. It takes time to set them up, which is why it's often best to start with a Google AdWords campaign first in order to test which keywords perform best for your niche.

Sounds Expensive!

Now, I can't blame you at this stage for thinking that registering large numbers of domain names and setting up blogs for each one would be expensive, time-consuming, and take a huge amount of maintenance, but the fact is it isn't and I'll explain why.

First of all, a domain name can have multiple subdomains; take for example the www.tilecleaning.co.uk domain referred to earlier. This is one domain, but has 19 subdomains, from http://ceramic.tilecleaning.co.uk all the way through to http://worktop.tilecleaning.co.uk. The same is true for the tiledoctor.biz website, which has 46 subdomains. That's 65 domains in total for the cost of two domain name registrations. There really is no logical limit on how many subdomains a domain can have. It's more a question of available server capacity; however, it's worth checking this with your chosen hosting company.

Secondly, 65 blogs does not mean 65 separate installations of WordPress, which in itself would be a big administrative overhead; backups would take forever, and upgrades to core files, themes, and plugins would be a constant activity. The fact is, WordPress can be configured to run in Multisite mode, which allows you to create multiple subdomain sites all from one installation of WordPress.

Lastly, because all of this work is done electronically, you can leverage the power of the internet and outsource the repetitive tasks to a country where the labour rates are far cheaper. Outsourcing is covered in depth in chapter 9.

Like any website, the main costs of this strategy are really incurred during the setup phase, where you may need some consultancy to get the site off the ground. Once it's running, maintenance is very low. The main expense will come from the time it takes to write articles to post on the sites; however, this task should only take 1 to 2 hours per day and could be outsourced or given to an existing member of staff.

The cost of an SBN strategy compares very favourably with Google AdWords—in fact, you can expect savings of around 70% and that's assuming you're running the AdWords campaign yourself and you haven't outsourced it to a certified professional, who will also be charging for their time.

Summary

Links are a very important part of getting your content to the top of the Google Search listing; however, you cannot rely on others to give you the links you need to achieve that. The only way to guarantee getting quality links is to be in control of the sites yourself and to do that, you need to create your own network of authority blogs that specialise in carefully selected topics and then use the power of social media to create more links. The result is a Social Blog Network.

CHAPTER 3

Keywords

Understanding which search words or phrases your customers are using when searching online is a fundamental part of online marketing. It makes sense, therefore, to spend time researching and identifying all the words and phrases your customers are likely to use before spending time and money on anything else.

You have to remember that a search engine is simply a computer that's reading the text on your web page. It's not intelligent enough to understand what the images on your page contain, nor does it understand much about the content of your page. It can, however, interpret the HTML tags in your web page to identify headers, bold words, and title tags to understand what the page is about. So, if your keywords are not highlighted in this way, you're sending the wrong message to the search engine.

Identifying Keywords

Keywords you should already be targeting in your marketing include:

Buyers' keywords – These are often used in conjunction with a product name or service when there is a serious intent to purchase. Examples include: *Best, Buy, Clearance, Discount, Guide, How to, New, Online, Repair, Review, Sale, Solution, Tutorial, Training, and Video.*

Common issues – These are common problems faced by your potential customers who are searching for solutions. Review customer emails and survey your staff to understand what these might be.

Names – This includes location place names, franchises, or areas and people relevant to your industry.

Products – This is the names of your products including generic names widely used in your business sector to identify them.

Chasing the Long Tail

If you're new to internet marketing, you will probably be tempted to go after the most obvious short keywords that match your niche. However, unless you're in a relatively new market, you will find that competition for these keywords is already quite tough, so it's best to avoid these at the beginning of your campaign and focus on the **low hanging fruit.**

To follow the strategy in this book, you will be publishing articles based around long combinations of keywords to target what is often referred to as the **long tail**. So instead of targeting "Weight Loss", which is a very popular search phrase with up to 1 million searches a month and is difficult to rank for naturally, you would look for something less popular and more specific such as "review of weight loss programs". One of the easiest ways to generate a long tail keyword is to add a location to the search phrase.

The next step is then to title your articles with the long tail phrase and include the keywords in the headings and text within the article.

Don't overuse keywords in your articles—keep it natural. Google uses a ratio of keywords to overall text in an article to decide its relevancy, known as **keyword density**. Google will penalise articles it considers are repeating keywords excessively.

Using this long tail approach will target less traffic; however, if you use this strategy to publish an article with a different long tail keyword combination each day, the traffic will soon mount up. Not only that, the traffic will also be more relevant to your niche.

For example, some previous articles Tile Doctor have published include:

- *Application of Anti-Slip Treatment at an Office Block*

- *Century-old Victorian Tiled Floor Rejuvenated in Finedon*

- *Cleaning a Block Paved Driveway in Hove*

- *Fantastic Black Brazilian Slate Tiles Rejuvenated in Thornton-Cleveleys*

- *Large Area of Limestone Tiled Flooring Burnished in Uckfield*

- *Limestone Tiled Floor Cleaning in Leatherhead*

- *Marble Entrance Hall Restored Through Burnishing in Congleton*

- *Varnished Brazilian Slate tiled floor refinished in Barrow-in-Furness*

- *Victorian and Quarry Tiled Floors Restored in Shrewsbury*

Notice how the titles contain typical search keywords such as the type of tile, activity being carried out, and the location? All of these are repeated in the body and headings within the actual article too.

Finding Keywords

One way of researching the most popular keywords related to your niche is to simply start typing in the Google Search bar. You will see that it automatically tries to guess what you're searching for by dropping down a list of the most popular related search phrases under the search box.

Whilst useful, you're going to need a lot more keywords than these few, so I recommend you make use of the free Google Keyword Planner tool, which comes built in to the Google AdWords platform. I've included the address below, but of course it may change:

https://adwords.google.com/ko/keywordplanner.

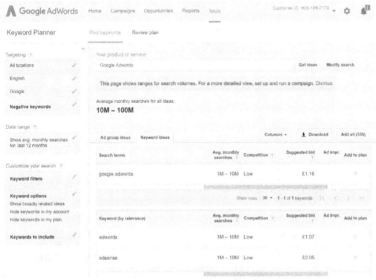

© 2015 Google Inc, used with permission. Google and the Google logo are registered trademarks of Google Inc.

If you're reading this book because of the title, it's probable that you're already familiar with AdWords and have been using it to advertise your business. If so, then great as you will already have done much of the required research. If not, then go ahead and create a free Google Account and explore.

To extract your existing keyword list from Google AdWords, look out for the Download button, which allow you to download keyword suggestions and keywords you have saved into an advertising plan.

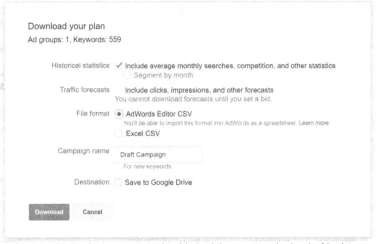

One thing you have to remember about the Google keyword tool is that the results you see come from the Google search platform, and although it's the most popular search engine, it's worth looking at other tools as well to get a complete picture. There are several other website tools that are worth looking at, some of which are mentioned in the following section.

KeywordTool.IO

Being able to work out keywords based on each search engine is a very useful feature, and www.keywordtool.io allows you to see what is popular on Google, YouTube, Bing and Amazon. You can also focus the search by country and language to build a better list targeted to your demographic.

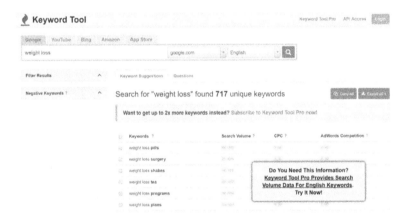

Like most of these tools, however, there are limitations on the free searches and you need to upgrade to the paid version to get the most from the service. This currently works out at $68 per month for the basic version, which includes search volume statistics. You will need these to understand which keywords are the most popular.

kwfinder.com

Keyword Finder is a very sophisticated yet easy to use service that not only provides keyword suggestions, it also analyses the competition so you can work out which keywords will be the easiest to rank for. Keywords can also be filtered by language and country. Again, like most of these tools, you really need to upgrade to the paid version to get the best out of it, as the free version restricts you to three keyword lookups per hour, which only offers you a taste.

At $12 a month for the basic version, it is cheaper than KeyWordTool.io; however, it's difficult to know how accurate the reported search volumes are in this tool, as this information is propriety and kept secret.

Another site worth taking a look at is www.moz.com/tools, who have a number of tools available with a free 30-day trial.

Summary

The idea at this point is to utilise the keyword tools and websites described previously to create a long list of unique keywords relevant to your business. I recommend you use a spreadsheet to compile the list and use the sorting facility to remove any duplicates. Once you have your list, save the spreadsheet for use later, as you will find it comes in very handy—especially when designing your own SBN solution and working out what topics you need to create content for.

CHAPTER 4

Web 2.0 and Social Media

In the early days of the internet, or Web 1.0 as it's commonly referred to, interaction between services was limited, and you really only had email, websites, and search to choose from. There were a few services such as Yahoo and CompuServe who combined these, but essentially these were just portals that brought information into a single location.

With the advent of YouTube, Facebook, Twitter, etc., Web 2.0 was born, and this brought in a new age of interaction with tools to share information easily between services and users. These more social tools have now become woven into our everyday lives, and if you're looking to reach an audience on the internet, it is by far the quickest way to do it.

Content is easily shared on these platforms and can soon spread across the internet like a virus (known as **"going viral"**). Search engines such as Google appreciate this and will see those shared links, which means more votes in the popularity contest and a higher ranking for the page. Naturally, social shares can get your message in front of a new audience, which of course will result in more traffic to your site.

Another advantage of these social tools is that many customers find it easier to share their experiences online, so by providing an official channel for this, it enables you to get closer to your customer and respond to that feedback (good or bad) in real time.

 When setting up your presence on social media, keep the design consistent and use similar profile photographs, @usernames, and cover images throughout. Ideally, your cover/header image should convey graphically what you're about, so use images relevant to your niche that are engaging and overlay it with your slogan and website URL.

The only downside to social media is that there are just so many platforms, and new ones keep appearing all the time. To be effective, you really need to have a presence on as many as possible.

Before we take a look at some of the most popular platforms, you need to be aware that there are five different categories: **Bookmarking, Blogging, Image Sharing, PDF Sharing**, and of course **Social Media**.

 **Blogging**

Blogs are a form of social media, as they allow users to leave comments on posts, which can be a good and a bad thing, as I'll explain shortly. There are several systems you can use to create blogs including the very popular WordPress. I highly recommend WordPress and have dedicated a whole chapter to it later in the book. Others include Blogger.com, Livejournal.com, Sett.com, and Tumblr.com. There are many others, but these are the most popular.

YouTube can also be considered as a blogging site, as you can post content and users can leave comments. However, due to its unique nature, I've included this under social media sites.

So, getting back to commenting, most blogs allow other people to specify a website URL when leaving a comment against a blog post, which is an ideal opportunity to generate a backlink. As a result, outsourcers are often tasked with seeking out blogs that allow comments and adding a comment with a link to the website they are currently promoting. Because of this, you will often see blogs posts, where the ability to comment has been left switched on, become abused with spammy comments.

Blog commenting is generally not a technique I would recommend giving to an outsourcer, as most comments are reviewed before being published and spammy comments are usually detected and deleted sooner or later.

To avoid being spammed, I recommend you switch blog commenting off for your own posts; however, before you do, there's no reason why you can't add your own useful comment and get a backlink to one of your own web pages first.

Malcolm Crowther on November 30, 2016 at 3:35 pm said: Edit

We recommend using a specialist cleaning product such as Tile Doctor Neutral Tile Cleaner for the regular cleaning of sealed tiles. Never use a steam cleaner on a sealed floor and if you wish to use another product always read the label in detail first, most supermarket tile cleaners are only suitable for ceramic tiles as many are acidic and this will erode and reduce the life of the sealer over time.

gloucester.tiledoctor.biz   Comments are closed.

Blog comments are, however, a great way of interacting with potential clients and starting conversations. So, if you do wish to leave blog commenting on but don't want the headache of having to monitor it for spam, take a look at www.disqus.com, who have developed a powerful system that can handle large volumes of comments.

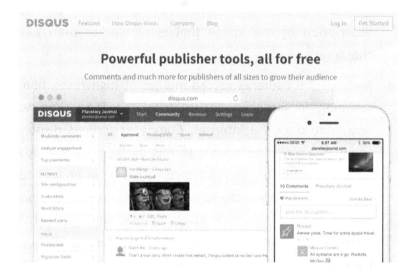

Image Sharing

I've mentioned previously that search engines are just large arrays of computers that know how to process text. This means they are unable to work out what an image represents, so they make a best guess based on the name of the image and the text that surrounds it. Being aware of this fact is very useful, as images are displayed in search results—so you really want your images to rank higher than others, as that in turn will lead to more visitors on your site.

You can maximise this opportunity by incorporating a few simple practices:

● Rename images with long titles, incorporating relevant keywords and hyphens to separate the words.

● Always populate the HTML alt tag with a concise description of the image that is no longer than 125 characters.

● Most digital cameras record images at high resolution, resulting in large images that take a long time to download over the internet. Computer screens display at much lower resolutions, so this detail is wasted. It's far more efficient, therefore, to resize large images to match the size they are to be displayed on screen. This makes them quicker to load without any noticeable difference in quality. To optimise images for use on websites take a look at www.optimizilla.com

● When reposting content in a blog that includes an image, refer to the image on the original site rather than uploading the image again, as even images can benefit from backlinks.

Image sharing is also a popular practice among web users, and like everything in this chapter, it's a great way to generate links back to your content. Think about it, how often have you shared an image on Facebook?

Back in 2004, Flickr was the original image sharing site; however, this was quickly superseded by Pinterest, which launched in 2010 and has become immensely popular.

 Pinterest

The great thing about Pinterest is it allows you to bookmark images (known as **pinning**) from around the web into collections called **boards**. These boards can be made public, and if someone else shares your passion, they can follow you and/or share your pins, all of which generates interest in what you're doing and creates backlinks to your site. Your goal should be to get all of your images pinned by users as much as possible, as each pin is a backlink that Google will see as more votes for your site.

This is quite a powerful idea, and it should not be underestimated as it has great potential for generating traffic. Naturally, this really only works if your niche lends itself to images, such as fashion, while this might not be the best channel for you if your niche is finance-related.

Pinterest has its own internal popular search engine that you can add your images to, and thereby encourages more re-pins. This is done by creating a Pinterest board for each topic being promoted and then loading that board with a large selection of related images that are visually engaging to the viewer. Large, bright images work best, and collages of images are also very popular.

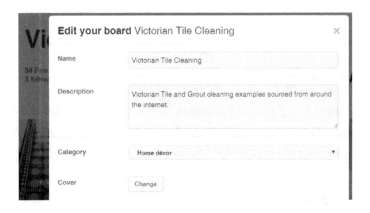

If you're struggling to find interesting images of your own, then add other people's images to your boards by pinning them.

When adding Pins from your own website, it's best to do this via the + button in the bottom right of the Pinterest window and choose *Save from a website*. This way, Pinterest will know and record where the image came from. This strategy also works with YouTube videos.

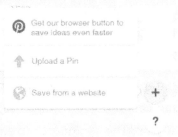

When setting up your boards, make sure you set an appropriate name, description, category, and cover image using keywords based around your selected topic, as this will help people find your boards when searching.

Although Pinterest doesn't have a search keyword planning tool available, you can still use the search auto-suggestion tool to work out what the most popular search terms are and then focus on those keywords.

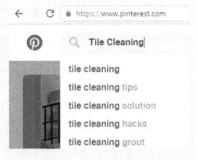

Like Twitter, it's not uncommon for people who you follow to follow you back, so one technique that increases visitors to your boards and increases re-pins is to search within Pinterest for people and boards using your keywords and then follow that person's followers. They will be alerted that you are following them and many will check you out and then follow you if they feel you have similar tastes.

Pinterest has a limit of 300 people you can follow in any hour, and if you exceed that, then Pinterest will alert you.

There are a number of tools that can help you make the best of Pinterest, and a few of the best are:

www.buffer.com	An image creation post scheduling tool that works with several social networks.
www.piktochart.com	An easy-to-use attention-grabbing image maker that is useful for creating infographics.
www.pingroupie.com	Find group boards on Pinterest where you can join and contribute with ease.
www.pinpinterest.com	Free tool with numerous useful functions that allow your Pinterest account to run on autopilot including Pin, Follow, Like, and Unfollow.
www.tailwindapp.com	Schedule posts, monitor conversations, see trending pins, launch promotions, and analyse results including competitors.
www.vizz.buzz	This creates stylised text-based images that can be used on social media to capture attention.

Social Networking

Social networking has hit the internet like a storm in the last 10 years, and social networks are great places to generate interest in your website. In fact, Facebook and YouTube are the second and third most popular websites on the Internet after Google.

 Facebook Pages

This platform has quickly become an absolute traffic generation goldmine, and with nearly two billion users, it's the most popular social platform on the planet. In order to take advantage of that, it makes sense to set up a Facebook page, or pages, where you can share your content as quickly as possible.

 A Facebook page should be used to promote a single product or service. Don't confuse the page's followers by posting unrelated content—use a different page for that. After all, there is no limit on the number of pages you can create in Facebook.

There are a number of different types of Facebook page you can create, so take your time and chose the one that's most relevant to what you're promoting on the page.

When setting up your page, fill in as much information as possible and include a profile and cover image to really make it stand out.

Add a *Learn More* call to action button that is linked to the related website. The *Learn More* option is far more likely to be clicked than the other options available, e.g. "Call Now", "Contact Us", "Send Message", "Sign Up" or "Send Email" etc.

The advertising features on Facebook are quite remarkable, and allow you to laser-target your advertising to just the right demographic. You can also build your own audience by uploading your contacts and then asking Facebook to add other members who fit the same profile (known as a

lookalike audience). A further option allows you to add a small piece of code (known as a **pixel**) to your website. This code links back to Facebook, which can match the IP address of the computer accessing the web page with a Facebook account and then display your advert to them the next time they log in.

Google AdWords has a similar re-targeting facility, both are quite powerful and provide a useful marketing technique that many people are unaware of. You can learn a lot more about these techniques from within the Google AdWords and Facebook Ad Manager screens.

Once set up, you can post introductions to your blog posts along with links and photographs. Ideally, you want to aim at driving customer engagement and getting your fans commenting on your post and sharing it with their friends. This in turn will drive further traffic to your blog and your website.

 Twitter

You might not be a fan of a Twitter, but it has some great benefits when it comes to internet marketing, so I recommend you set up an account. At the very least, it's an international directory/research tool that allows you to locate other people and businesses in your niche quite easily. The trending feature also allows you to see which topics are generating interest right now, and may give you some idea what to blog about.

Messages on Twitter are known as **tweets** and currently have a limit of 140 characters, so each message needs to be carefully crafted to ensure you get the most out of the limited word count.

Communication on Twitter essentially breaks down to @usernames and #hashtags. To tweet directly to someone, include the @username in the tweet. To join the conversation, simply add the #hashtag. Sounds simple, I know, but it's extremely effective. It's been said that to tweet without including a hashtag is Twitter suicide.

One thing you should keep in mind is that a Twitter feed can feel like driving at high speed—everything moves so fast, meaning your post will flash past and probably never be seen. This means it's important to direct your posts to a specific audience by including @usernames and #hashtags. To decide which #hashtags are likely to be the most popular, do some research on hashtags.org.

Building Followers

To build your list of followers on Twitter, search for posts using your niche-related keywords. Scroll through the posts and look for accounts that have lots of active followers and then follow them. Chances are, if they are following someone in your niche, they will follow you back—

especially if you have previously tweeted niche-related information. Twitter is on the lookout for accounts that overuse this technique, so never follow more than 100 other accounts per day. Additionally, they put a limit on the ratio of accounts you can follow in relation to the number of users following you, so use a tool such as www.crowdfireapp.com to regularly remove users who have not followed you back.

Crowdfire is a useful site, and there are many others that allow you to maximise your use of Twitter. Here are some others worth taking a look at:

www.adretweet.com	This is a Twitter marketplace where you can buy retweets, comments, followers, favourites, and sponsored tweets for around $6.
www.howdoigetfollowers.net	A service where you can buy Twitter followers and retweets, Instagram followers and likes, Facebook fans and likes, and YouTube video views and likes. Prices start from $27

www.manageflitter.com	A Twitter Management service designed to grow your followers and optimise your use of Twitter. There is a limited free service available, and access to the full features set costs $49 per month.
www.twitteraudit.com	A free service that will analyse a Twitter account's followers and report how may are fake accounts. Very useful if you are considering paying someone to tweet to their followers.
www.tweetdeck.com	A free Twitter dashboard that makes managing your Twitter account easier.
www.twellow.com	A free service that locates Twitter accounts via relevant business categories or in your area.

www.twitaholic.com	A free service that scans Twitter regularly to determine who has the most followers.
www.twitdom.com	This is a directory of over 2,000 Twitter applications.
www.twuffer.com	A tweeting service that allows you to queue up tweets and schedule when they are posted. The free service allows 50 tweets per month, the unlimited service is $5.99 per month.

If you can't find a tool that you need, then there is an **API** to Twitter that gives you full access to the platform, allowing you to search and tweet via your own scripts. I've used it myself to create a script that automatically tweets testimonials from customers of Tile Doctor.

Getting Publicity with Retweets

If you're launching a new website, then Twitter can be a great way to generate some free publicity. The first step is to search Twitter for people related to a particular keyword or niche. In the following example, we launched a new site to target the UK county of Cornwall, so we searched for "Cornwall" and clicked on the *People* tab, which returned 102 relevant Twitter accounts.

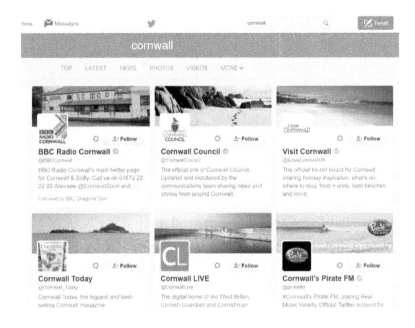

The next step is to send an individual tweet to each of the accounts you feel are relevant to your niche using their Twitter @username. If you make it individual, it's more likely to get attention than a broadcast to numerous accounts.

Check whether a Twitter account is active by clicking on the account to see when the last post was made. There are many accounts that have been simply forgotten about and never deleted.

TileProf @TileDoctorUK · 45m
@bopproperty Introducing Dave Worth from #Bude our Tile, Grout & Stone Cleaning specialist covering your county bit.ly/2gejYU0

TileProf @TileDoctorUK · 46m
@Cornwall_Prop Introducing Dave Worth from #Bude our Tile, Grout & Stone Cleaning specialist covering your county bit.ly/2gejYU0

Most of these Twitter accounts are constantly on the lookout for fresh material to tweet about, so you're in with a good chance of your message being retweeted to their followers. In the following example, @Cornwall_Info did exactly that and re-tweeted our message to their 18,700 followers.

Cornwall Information
@Cornwall_Info

Comish based info, news, photos, videos
from The Duchy - likes to share a sense
of place with Cornwall's people & visitors.

 Google Plus

Google is without a doubt the leader among the search providers, so if they do something, it's a good idea to get on board! This includes Google Plus (Google+), which was started as a rival to Facebook but never really took off in the same way.

Google+ has features called Collections and Communities, which work in a similar way to Facebook Pages and Facebook Groups. Both can be particularly useful for showcasing your work.

Google, like Facebook, has implemented a privacy feature to limit who can see your posts. Make sure you select *Public* during the setup process as you cannot change this later.

For Tile Doctor, we made sure each member of the network had their own Google+ account and every blog post was copied into the related Google+ account feed.

Dirty Victorian Hallway Floor Cleaning Westcliffe on Sea - http://south ...

https://plus.google.com/107321937334500112473/posts/HPm4LiQsRNV ▾
Nick Murphy

5 days ago - ... http://south-essex.tiledoctor.biz/dirty-victorian-hallway-floor-cleaning-westcliffe-on-sea/ Dirty Victorian Hallway Floor **Cleaning** Westcliffe on Sea | South Essex ...

Slate Tile Cleaning and Grout Recolouring in a Linwood Kitchen - http ...

https://plus.google.com/115573116375967044838/posts/bK8fs7P78qH ▾
Steve Thomson

9 Nov 2016 - Slate **Tile Cleaning** and Grout Recolouring in a Linwood Kitchen -
http://glasgow.tiledoctor.biz/slate-tile-cleaning-and-grout-recolouring-in-a-linwood-kitchen/

http://lancashire.tiledoctor.co.uk/ Grout Cleaning and Colouring ...

https://plus.google.com/110983965910505625322/posts/Cr4gcRi5Xz3 ▾
Russell Taylor

12 Dec 2014 - http://**lancashire**.tiledoctor.co.uk/ **Grout Cleaning** and Colouring Bathroom
Wall **Tiles** in Preston I recently paid a visit to a customer at a house in the town of Preston ...

Google's products are integrated into their search platform, so for maximum exposure, it makes sense to jump on board. In fact, you usually find that posts from Google+ appear in search results way ahead of other content.

As well as adding your photograph or logo and cover picture to your Google+ profile, it's a good idea to add the URL of your blog and any other sites you contribute to. Remember, Google counts links as popularity votes, so take advantage. To do this, simply click the pink + button at the bottom of the *About Me* page and click the *Sites* option. When the

Sites window appears, add the URL of your blog to the *Contributor* to section and click OK.

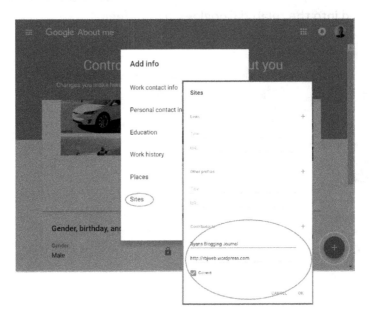

The caveat with Google+ is that it's less popular than Facebook, which has over a billion users. However, as with anything made by Google it's still worth serious consideration and you may find that your potential customers already have a thriving community on the platform.

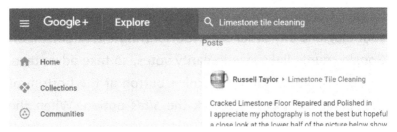

 **YouTube**

Producing your own videos has never been easier or cheaper. With services such as YouTube, everyone has the ability to create their very own TV channel or video blog (**vlog**). With the launch of Google Chromecast, you can also watch YouTube on most televisions, so not only can you watch hundreds of terrestrial, cable, and satellite channels, you can also subscribe to thousands of YouTube channels. This makes video even more attractive for those looking to get their message across.

Video Creation

The easiest way to create videos is with the free Movie Maker application that comes with the Windows and Apple operating systems. You can also create photo streaming videos with captions that showcase the work or product. It's a very straightforward process, and if you have hired a full-time outsourcer, then this is a great task for them to complete.

Once the video is ready, give it a relevant name containing your keywords and upload it to YouTube. Ensure the URL of the website being promoted is in the first line of the text box, and add some relevant text containing more of your keywords. Don't forget that each video provides a backlink to your website. There are more tips to getting your video ranked later in the chapter. If you're looking to create something more sophisticated and make your videos look really professional, you should learn how to use Final Cut Pro or Sony Vegas Pro. Or as an intermediate step, use HitFilm 4 Express, a free video editor available for both Apple and PC that is fully loaded with functionality. To get more information about any of these products look for videos about them on YouTube which is a great source of training material.

 I highly recommend that you use outsourcers for tasks such as video creation and submission. Hiring outsourcers is covered in detail in Chapter 9.

There are many resources you can use to create videos including the websites below:

www.animoto.com	Video/slideshow creation software that works on both PC and Mac.
www.camstudio.org	This records screen and audio activity on your PC. It's great for creating how-to videos.
www.makewebvideo.com	Create low-cost videos fast from templates including Explainer, Whiteboard, Corporate, and Cartoon.

www.mandy.com	A comprehensive guide to independent film/TV production resources.
www.techsmith.com/download/jing	Free but limited screen recording software for PC and Mac.
www.telestream.net/screenflow/overview.htm	Video editing software for Mac.
www.veeroll.com	Generate stunning video ads automatically.
www.videoblocks.com	Find studio-quality, affordable stock footage, motion backgrounds, after-effects templates, and more.

You can also use audio and video from other sources; however, be wary of breaching copyright, especially when adding audio to your own movies, and seek permission if in doubt.

YouTube Strategy

Google owns YouTube and understands that many of its search engine users would prefer to watch rather than read, so it includes one or two videos in its search results. These are usually quite high up on the first results page, most likely right at the start. Your strategy should therefore be to get your video into this prime slot for your chosen keywords. If you follow some of the advice here, this is not as difficult as it sounds.

First, we need to establish the factors that affect the popularity of videos on YouTube. Please remember that only Google knows exactly how their algorithm works; however, the following are well-known as being highly influential factors.

Likes	Likes are an indication of popularity and will improve a video's ranking for a keyword. Many **vloggers** openly encourage their viewers to click the *Like* button as part of their video.
Links	Google loves links (it counts them as votes, especially those from authority sites), so do encourage viewers to link and share your video.
Comments	Lots of comments are another signal that a video is engaging and popular among viewers.
Playlists	YouTube allows users to bookmark videos into Playlists or Watch Later lists, which are further signals that a video is popular.

Social shares	YouTube provides tools for you to share your video, and being part of the Google network, it's able to track the video's popularity.
Subscribers	This is a big signal that your channel is popular— and this will affect the ranking of **all** the videos on the channel.
Viewer duration	YouTube is able to determine how much of a video users are watching, and it ranks videos that have been watched fully over those that haven't. With this in mind, it makes sense to publish shorter videos as they are more likely to be watched to the end, and split long videos into shorter episodes.
Views	YouTube tracks the number of times a video has been watched. The more views a video gets, the stronger the indication that it contains popular content, which should be promoted.

So, to get your videos ranking high for your target keywords, it's just a matter of identifying your competition and then exceeding the number of channel subscribers, likes, links, views, and so on that they have. Again, this is a task that can be outsourced quite cheaply. Fiverr.com in particular offers many services for exactly that purpose. You will find more information on using Fiverr in Chapter 9, which covers outsourcing in detail.

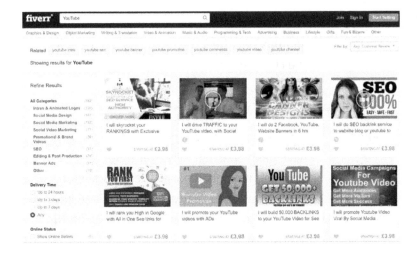

Remember **long tail search**, which was mentioned in the Keyword chapter? It's difficult to rank easily for the most popular keywords, so aim to create lots of videos on less popular keywords as they are easier to target.

To identify the low hanging fruit, simply type your keywords into YouTube and take a look at the top ten videos. Create a spreadsheet listing the main factors for each video such as channel subscribers, views, likes, and comments. Look for low numbers that can be surpassed with your own videos. If it's not obvious why a video is ranking higher, then it's probably due to external factors such as the number of links pointing to it.

 **Instagram**

Acquired by Facebook in 2012, Instagram is an extremely popular and growing online mobile photo and short video sharing social network service. Its roots are in mobile photo sharing, where it has a huge fan base of 500 million active users with 90% under the age of 35, so it's an ideal platform to target the younger generation. The platform is free, so there should be no reason not to include it in your social portfolio and start a following.

Naturally, being a photo sharing platform, you need to focus on creating inviting images that capture the viewer's attention and encourage them to learn more and visit your site. Instagram comes with a number of graphic tools that can help you with this, or you can create your own using a website such as pablo.buffer.com or www.befunky.com.

Before and after transformations work well, as do inspirational quotes, short punchy testimonials, and special offers. With each image posted, you can also supply up to 2,200 characters of text, so it makes sense to fill this up with text from a related blog post and relevant hashtags to make the content more searchable.

Like Twitter and Pinterest, one way of attracting followers is to like and comment on other user's posts. Any curious person will want to see who has engaged with them, and if they like what they see, they will follow you back. There's even a service that will do this for you called instagress.com. It's easy to set up and has a 3-day free trial available, after which it's $9.99 a month.

Bookmarking and PDF Sharing

To generate more links back to your content, look at using Bookmarking and PDF Sharing services. The influence of these services on the Google search algorithm is low; however, a link is a link, so if you can add your site to these services easily, it's worth doing.

Bookmarking

With over a billion websites and who knows how many web pages, trying to make sense of the internet can be challenging. Of course, web browsers allow you to bookmark sites that interest you; however, the trouble is that you can't share those lists between computers or with your contacts. Like everything to do with the internet, of course there is a solution, and this comes in the form of bookmarking services like that offered by Delicious.

Delicious (https://del.icio.us) allows you to install a small button in your browser. To bookmark a site, you hit the button and a form pops up asking you what tags to apply, so you can categorise the link and easily find it again later.

The interesting thing about this is that you can make your bookmarked links public, so anyone can see them, including search engines. This means more links and more votes in the Google search engine.

Other Bookmarking services include Bitly.com, Diigo.com, Folkd.com, Linkagogo.com, Instapaper.com, Plurk.com, Reddit.com, Scoop.it, Stumbleupon.com, and Zotero.org.

PDF Sharing

There are a number of services available that will convert your web pages into PDF documents, store them, and share them publicly. Companies that do this include Docdroid.net, Issuu.com, ge.tt, Scribd.com, and Sendspace.com.

The reason this is useful is because PDF documents are similar to web pages in that they comprise text that is formatted using a mark-up language. Google has the ability to read this text and often includes PDF documents in its index.

Summary

In this chapter, we touched on some of the most common social platforms available on the internet today, there are many others and new ones are being created all the time. In all cases, they provide an easy way to create links back to a website and give you another opportunity to promote the site or service to a different audience.

To help maintain the look and feel of your presence on social platforms aim to use similar cover images that display your message, logo and contact information. If you need help creating cover images take a look at the service provided by www.socialcover.graphics.

Only Google can say exactly how much influence links from social platforms have on the Google algorithm, but there certainly is strong evidence to support the fact that social shares have a part to play—and can undoubtedly increase the chance of potential customers coming across your content.

CHAPTER 5

Creating and Posting Content

Before you start designing your own SBN solution, the most important factor you need to consider is what content you will be able to create. Let's face it, there's no point creating a blog without having anything to publish in it. If you're struggling for inspiration, take a look at some of the following strategies to generate content:

Activities - You may need to be a little inventive and it may require a few staff incentives, but it's very easy to create content based around the everyday activities happening within your business. With these posts, you're not looking to publish well-researched articles, but to think more like a journalist with a deadline to make the front page. The objective should be to get as many pages in the search engines as possible.

Competitors - If you're short on ideas for content, take a look at what your competitors are blogging about. I'm not suggesting that you plagiarise their posts, but some of their ideas may give you inspiration. If your competition isn't posting much at all on their websites, then that's good news as they will soon be losing a lot of their business to you.

Events - If your niche has a number of key events or relevant dates, post a calendar at the start of each month and then follow it up with a post about each event as it happens.

Facts, figures, customer surveys - With a little research, you should be able to track down statistical information about your chosen niche that you can re-publish on a regular basis; just remember to quote your source. Ideally, you should publish relevant information from within the organisation or customer surveys and pre-announce its publication by listing it in the events diary.

How-to guides - You can really go to town and have some fun with one, essentially providing the reader with a list of instructions that will make the completion of a niche-related activity easy to follow.

Interviews - Free publicity is always welcome, so set up interviews with relevant people in your niche or people within your organisation. The interview can easily be conducted over the phone, recorded, and then transcribed. I've used MP3 Skype Recorder on the PC to do this previously; Skype maintain a full list of compatible software providers on the following web page:

https://support.skype.com/en/faq/FA12395/how-can-i-record-my-skype-calls.

There are a number of low cost transcription services available including https://www.rev.com/transcription, which costs $1 per minute.

News alerts - Create a Google News alert so you are notified when a new story breaks in your niche. To do this, visit https://news.google.co.uk and search for your topic, then scroll down to the bottom of the screen and click the Create alert button. Even if you don't wish to use the news for a full article, it can make great fodder for your social media posts.

Reviews - Reviewing relevant products, books, videos, events, and so on will provide engaging content for your blog.

Top Ten - Top ten posts are where you list ten related items and rank them in order, along with your justification. It's an old marketing trick that's been around since the year dot, but it works.

Testimonials - As we discussed earlier, social proof is an extremely important part of the sales process, and you should already be collating and displaying testimonials on your site, ideally from an independent source. Why not compress a number of these into a single blog post (see chapter 8 on Reputation Marketing for more on this topic).

To maximise the SBN strategy, you really need to post at least one 500-word article every day. So, make sure your chosen subject matter is a wide enough topic to support this.

Authority Sites

Basically, an SBN is just a whole host of blogs that link between each other; however, to get the most power out of the network, each blog needs to have its own individual identity and contain a large number of posts on the same subject matter—only then will Google see it as an authority on that subject. Designing an SBN, therefore, is a simple matter of arranging the keyword list you created in chapter 3 into related groups and then registering a domain name for each blog network.

To see how a multiple blog marketing solution could be implemented in practise, we'll take a look at some examples starting with a franchise business.

Franchise Example

ChipsAway are a typical franchise company based in the UK. They have over 200 franchisees and offer the following services:

- Alloy wheel refinishing

- Bumper scuff repair

- Minor dents and scratch repairs

ChipsAway, like most companies with blogs, have a site where they post a researched article around once a week (www.chipsaway.co.uk/our-world/blog/). In the past, their posts included "UK's Top 10 Most Popular Car Colours" and "How to Care for Your Paintwork in the Winter". Often you find titles like these are produced by marketing execs who are tasked with producing relevant stories every week.

The trouble is that whilst I'm sure a lot of work and research goes into these weekly blog posts, Google (being a computer) is unable to analyse the post for quality—it merely uses links to determine what is popular and therefore worth reading. So, to gain more exposure in

Google, ChipsAway need to produce a new article every day. They can then create links to each post on all of their social media accounts.

ChipsAway do have a web page for each of their franchisees; however, it's more of a directory, with each page containing similar information to the next

(https://www.chipsaway.co.uk/local/).

To follow the successful strategy implemented at Tile Doctor, ChipsAway could get their IT and Marketing teams to set up a blog for each of their franchisees detailing the area they cover and testimonials. They could then add lots of detail and photographs of their exploits. This alone would create 200 websites from aberdeen.chipsaway.co.uk to york.chipsaway.co.uk, all pointing back to the main website. This will generate a huge amount of web pages, link juice, and traffic that will drown out the competition in the search engines.

Additionally, they could create three authority blogs (one for each core service) containing only articles relating to those services. Then if they add more car repair services to their portfolio, they could add more to the authority blogs, such as upholstery cleaning. Each blog would contain a front page detailing relevant products and advice. The posts on these sites would provide details of real-world examples, including photographs of completed work by their operatives—all linking back to the original post on the operative's blog. Of course, each blog would also be connected to their social media accounts to generate even more backlinks.

 Alternative Energy Company Example

The alternative energy market has huge growth potential and this has not gone unnoticed, leading to a big increase in competition. This is not an unusual scenario—and it affects many businesses, where they see new competition flush with large investor-led marketing budgets appear, ready to take a bite out of their market share.

The one advantage that an older company has over a new company—but that is rarely exploited—is its existing customer base, which is usually full of happy customers who would be eager to share their story. So, for an area with huge competition such as alternative energy, they could set up a series of blogs, one for each technology such as Solar Panels, Bio Mass Boilers, Heat Pumps, etc.

They would then start publishing their stories along with photographs and estimated savings. Not only does this give the company more exposure online, but it also provides a great source of social proof that can be used by the sales force along with testimonials.

Travel Company Example

The internet has become a huge market for travel companies. According to the Google AdWords keyword tool, the keywords "Holiday" and "Vacation" each receive between one and ten million searches every month worldwide. As a result, the competition is immense. With some very big companies who have equally-large budgets operating in this market, using a low-cost blogging campaign is a great way to level the field.

You may argue that TripAdvisor has already covered this by quickly becoming the number one review site for holidays; however, it's a very large niche and all this proves is that there is a huge demand for more information about destinations—something a blog can deliver in a far better quality format.

If you're in the travel niche, blogging presents a great way of providing information to potential customers. Video also works particularly well in this niche and can be integrated into blog posts quite easily.

To get recognised as an authority site by Google, you could set up a host of blogs for each destination/attraction and incentivise every customer with discount vouchers off their next holiday for every story published.

Holidaymakers love taking photographs, so it shouldn't be too difficult to get them to help you generate a huge volume of blog posts; it just takes a little imagination to get the formula right.

 There is already a huge number of travel-related blogs and YouTube videos about travel destinations. As long as you give credit to the author, you can reproduce these posts for free on your site.

Restaurant Example

Most restaurants tend to have very static sites with pages for location, menu, contact information, and pictures of the restaurant. Like most websites, this really only conveys the features of the product, rather than selling it to the consumer.

To turn this around, the customer needs to be able to feel immersed in the ambiance of the restaurant and have confidence that the service and the food is second to none. The chef's reputation is a key element of this, so a separate blog detailing the chef's favourite recipes, colourful photographs, and short video interviews of the chef cooking would make compelling content. It will generate its own traffic and result in visitors linking across to the restaurant to make a booking. The restaurant itself could also post about special occasions that took place in the restaurant, with photographs of happy customers enjoying the service.

While this is a smaller example than that of a franchise, the same principles of using multiple blogs and social media to create links still applies. The principle of an SBN can easily be scaled to suit, and naturally if you're running a small business, then you will struggle to generate the content required to feed your blogs daily. However, you can still make progress by maximising your web presence with blog posts, adding as much content as you can and ensuring that content is syndicated via social media across the web. Creating and sharing content in this manner increases your footprint in the Google index and helps you get found online.

 Accountant Example

When it comes to blogging, accountants really do have it easy! If you're an accountant, although you can't breach your clients' confidentiality, there is tons of relevant news being published by the government that you can put your own spin on. There's also a number of different taxes and business sectors you can write about.

The same strategies discussed earlier apply here too—you can create multiple blogs and incentivise your staff with bonuses to create the material, cross-publishing the stories across other sites and social media as you go. In this case, each department within the accountancy firm would have their own blog and their posts would be republished on another authority site, or even sites.

I could go on and on with examples of how you can implement this strategy for all sorts of businesses, but hopefully by now you get the idea.

Paid Content

It's worth bearing in mind that the internet is full of writers and service companies happy to write content for you, so if creating content is not something you are able to do in-house, then look at paying someone else to do it. You will find more information and resources on how to go about this in chapter 9, which covers outsourcing.

Summary

A number of approaches that you can use to create content for your blogs were discussed. It's the content that will generate the backlinks you need to get your sites ranking higher in Google; it's a key part of the SBN strategy and so it's worth spending some time now brainstorming your own ideas before moving onto the next chapter.

Remember, you're looking for a journalistic approach to your content, not research; the SBN strategy is about publishing a large number of posts with a minimum of 500 words and a good mix of your keywords.

CHAPTER 6

WordPress

Since its creation in 2003, WordPress has grown to become the most popular tool for building websites and controlling their content. This is because it's very intuitive, easy to install, easy to learn, and hides complexity well. It's also extremely configurable, with a wealth of low-cost themes available that enable you to quickly change the look and feel to suit your purpose.

Being popular also means there are a lot of people out there worldwide who know how to use it, so it's very easy to recruit the talent you need to get a site launched and configured exactly the way you want it. There are also many books and training resources available should you wish to learn it yourself.

WordPress is constantly evolving, and one of the most powerful features was launched in version 3.0—"Multisite". This feature enables you to create a network of WordPress sites under a single domain. Once configured, it allows you to create a new WordPress blog on the same installation in seconds (later in this chapter, you'll see how to install Multisite).

 Windows or Linux? In my experience, Linux servers have proved to be a far more reliable and secure for website hosting than Windows servers, which have to be constantly patched with updates to keep them one step ahead of the hackers. Additionally, Multisite web hosting only works correctly on Linux hosting, so it's got to be Linux.

CAUTION: The following section details how to install WordPress on a server, so it does get technical. However, WordPress is a popular system, so if this is not your thing, feel free to skip this chapter and hire someone to do this.

Installing WordPress

WordPress is famous for its simple, five-minute installation, and many hosting companies offer it as a "ready to install" option in the control panel, so in most cases, it should just be a question of clicking a button.

The alternative is to download the latest source code from the WordPress.org site (https://wordpress.org/download/) and install it manually.

There are a huge amount of guides and book on installing WordPress, including the official WordPress instructions (https://codex.wordpress.org/installing_wordpress).

So rather than repeating the instructions, we'll focus on recommended changes that will ensure you get the best SEO value from your site.

I don't recommend you install a blog on the same domain as your main website, Google will see any links between the two as internal, which carries less weight than an external link.

Once installed, you need to choose a theme that will define the overall look and feel of your site. There are literally thousands to choose from, including a large selection of free themes recommended by WordPress:

https://en-gb.wordpress.org/themes/

There are also thousands of paid themes available, so it's worth browsing one of the better theme sites such as Template Monster before making a decision:

https://www.templatemonster.com/wordpress-themes.php.

Template Monster groups every theme into relevant business categories, from art through to travel, making it very easy to navigate and browse themes that are relevant to your niche. With non-exclusive licenses from around $45, it's a very cheap way of getting the right look for your website.

Installing Multisite

Something that many of the guides and manuals about WordPress don't cover is how to set up the Multisite feature, which allows you to host multiple blogs on the same installation. I'll touch on the steps required now, but they may change over time, so I recommend you follow the full instructions to safely activate this feature in the WordPress codex, which you can find at:

https://codex.wordpress.org/create_a_network.

Step 1. Edit wp-config.php

The first step requires you to add a line to the end of the wp-config.php file, which is found in the root of the WordPress directory. WordPress is built on the PHP scripting language, which is text-based, so any text editor will be able to open the file. However, you should find that your website control panel provides the ability to edit it directly over the internet. Naturally, this will depend on which hosting company you have signed up with.

 You should always make a backup of the wp-config.php file before making any changes.

Most recent installations of WordPress already have an entry for the control parameter WP_ALLOW_MULTISITE, and you can just switch the parameter value from false to true. If it's missing, just add the following lines:

/* Multisite */

define('WP_ALLOW_MULTISITE', true);

Save this change and then access the WordPress installation control panel in your web browser. If it's already open, simply refresh the browser. If it's done correctly, you should find that you have a new Network Setup option listed under the Tools menu.

Step 2. Disable Plugins

Before being able to configure the network settings, you may be asked to deactivate any plugins that have been installed.

Deactivating plugins is easily done from the Plugins page, and any configuration information will not be deleted during deactivation.

Step 3. Configure Network Settings

With the plugins deactivated, the network setup page will change and allow you to click the blue Install button at the bottom of the page.

Step 4. Configure config and htaccess files

The page will then refresh and ask you to make some changes to your wp-config.php and .htaccess files, which you should be able to do via your web hosting control panel as before. The .htaccess file will be located in the root of your root of your website, but the config.php file will be in the WordPress installation directory.

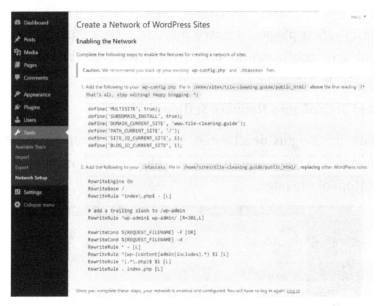

I also recommend you add the following setting to the wp-config.php file:

```
define('NOBLOGREDIRECT', 'http://www.tile-cleaning.guide/' );
```

This will ensure that any unrecognised web page request returns the user to the mentioned site and that they are not given a missing page error.

Step 5. Re-enable plugins

Once complete, reload your browser, log back in to the site, and re-activate the plugins—and you're done.

The site administration panel will look slightly different, but you now have a new My Sites menu available that will allow you to create multiple websites under the same domain.

Configuring WordPress

Once your installation is live, there are several settings you should configure to reduce maintenance and improve SEO. Unsurprisingly, you will find all these settings in the WordPress menu under Settings.

Blog commenting is a strategy used to generate backlinks; however, unless you have a particularly viral story that encourages a good discussion, you will find that most comments come from other internet marketers looking for backlinks, so it's best to disable this option for the general public.

Other comment settings ☐ Comment author must fill out name and email

☑ Users must be registered and logged in to comment (Signup has been disabled. Only members of this site can comment.)

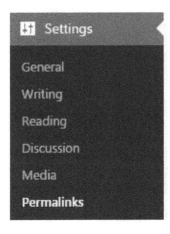

The Permalinks setting defines the structure of the URL for pages published on the site; by default, you will find it is set to a series of numbers, resulting in each page being referenced with a meaningless number. Numbers do nothing to boost the SEO value of your posts, so this should be changed to *Post name* as soon as possible.

Common Settings

○ Plain	http://lancashire.tiledoctor.biz/?p=123
○ Day and name	http://lancashire.tiledoctor.biz/2017/01/07/sample-post/
○ Month and name	http://lancashire.tiledoctor.biz/2017/01/sample-post/
○ Numeric	http://lancashire.tiledoctor.biz/archives/123
⦿ Post name	http://lancashire.tiledoctor.biz/sample-post/

Widgets

Most WordPress themes allow you to create a sidebar and footer very easily and populate those areas with elements known as widgets, many of which are installed by default, while others can be added by installing the required plugin. Widgets offer a great opportunity to add static and dynamic content to your pages, such as the following:

- Use the Recent Posts widget to give visitors quick access to the latest posts on the site. This is also a great way of generating a menu of internal links which will be appreciated by Google. The widget is configurable to control the number of posts displayed and whether to display the post date.

  RECENT POSTS
  - Cracked Mexican Terracotta Kitchen Tiles Restored in Ormskirk February 6, 2017
  - Restoring Eight Bathrooms at Self-Catering Cottages in County Meath February 3, 2017

- The Social Profiles widget can be configured to show icons for many different social platforms and provide visitors with a quick link to your content on social media. To add this to your list of available options, install the plugin via the link below:

  CONNECT WITH US

  https://wordpress.org/plugins/social-profiles-widget/

There are a large number of plugins that will add buttons for your social media accounts to your web pages. You may find that your chosen theme already comes with the ability to do this built-in—either way it's essential that you get them added to your site.

- The Text widget allows you to enter text, including HTML, which is especially useful for integrating with other web services such as opt-in forms and testimonials, or simply just displaying a logo or image.

- You can use the Categories, Custom Menu, Pages, or Links widgets to provide users with a quick way to navigate within the website.

- The Calendar widget adds a diary to the sidebar, allowing the user to select posts by publication date.

- The RSS widget is a very useful option that allows you to list posts from other blogs. RSS is quite a big topic so I've covered it in detail in the next section.

Other widgets will be available depending on the theme and other plugins that you have installed.

RSS Feeds

RSS, or Really Simple Syndication, is a method of distributing content using structured XML, and all blogging sites have this feature. You don't need to concern yourself with the technicalities, but essentially rather than visiting multiple blogs every day, you can aggregate all the feeds from each blog into a single news reader. There's a lot of choice when it comes to news reader software, and apps are available on all platforms, including smartphones.

There are services available that allow you to combine the feeds from the multiple blogs in your SBN into a single feed that can then be displayed in the sidebar of each website using the RSS widget.

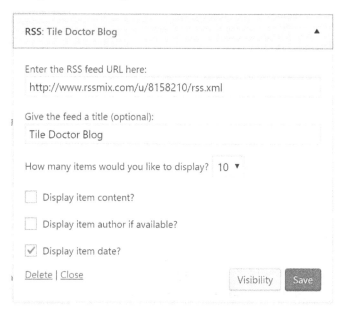

For example, this screenshot shows the RSS news widget for Tile Doctor, which is configured to show the last 10 posts in the sidebar. You will notice that the URL shown is not from a Tile Doctor site, but from rssmix.com—a free service that does the work of aggregating multiple RSS feeds into one.

Another great feature about RSS is that most news sites publish an RSS feed, including the BBC and Google News, which you can easily display in the sidebar of your WordPress blog using the RSS widget. Google provides instructions on how to do this via its search engine.

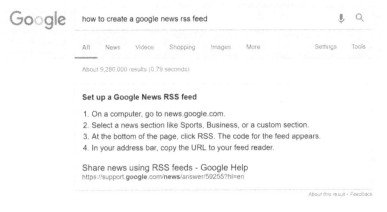

Essential WordPress Plugins

WordPress allows you to extend its functionality extensively by installing plugins, and the plugins listed here are highly recommended.

Social Link Machine v2.0

Before I discovered this plugin, I used to have my outsourcer spend time every day posting links to articles across multiple social media channels including Google+, Pinterest, Twitter, etc. With this plugin installed on every WordPress site, this work has now been reduced to specific promotions, while the plugin takes care of the rest automatically.

The plugin is only $47 for the unlimited version which allows you to use the plugin on multiple WordPress installations. $47 is excellent value when you consider how powerful it is and how much work would be needed if you wanted to do the same job manually.

The plugin has numerous features for auto-sharing your content across social media including the ability to integrate with external content spinning software such as thebestspinner.com and spinrewriter.com, services that re-organise the text in each post to make them look unique. A word of warning here though, Google is looking for naturally created content and frowns on the use of content spinners so I would not advise their use.

Another integration option allows you to connect to services from backlinksindexer.com, indexification.com, and instantlinkindexer.com, which use various methods to ensure all your social posts get ranked within Google.

A further integration option allows you to automatically bring in content from external sources including RSS feeds from other blogs or articlebuilder.net, which generates unique highly-spun articles in a large range of niches from Acid Reflux to Yeast Infections, again I advise against the use of automatically generated content as it goes against Google guidelines.

To set up the plugin, it needs to be configured with the details of your social media accounts. Then, every time you create a post, the plugin re-posts it on those platforms. You should find the names of these services familiar as they were detailed in chapter 4 on Web 2.0 and social media. The accounts take between two and ten minutes to set up and are well worth creating, as each one will create a valuable backlink for every post you publish.

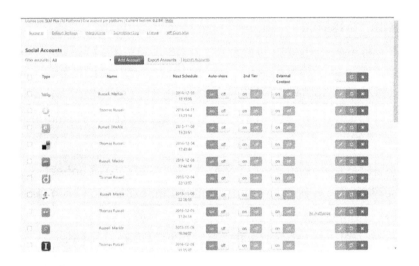

This screenshot shows the configuration page for the plugin, which works with up to 32 social media services in the categories of Document Sharing through to Social Networking. There's a full list of all the supported platforms on the next page.

Bookmarking Sites

- Bitly
- Delicious
- Deviantart
- Diigo
- Folkd
- Linkagogo
- Instapaper
- Plurk
- Reddit
- Scoop.it
- Stumbleupon
- Zotero

PDF Sharing

- Docdroid
- Issuu
- Gett
- Scribd
- Sendspace

Image Sharing

- Flickr
- Pinterest

Social Networking

- Facebook
- Google+
- Twitter
- Xing
- Youtube

Web 2.0 Blogs

- Blog.com
- Blogger
- Livejournal
- Overblog
- Sett
- Tumblr
- Wordpress-based
- Wordpress.com

Cron Control

Again, this is very technical, so you may want to outsource this task. Social Link Machine and other services rely on a set of plugins called "Cron Schedules" and "WP-Cron-Control" to execute and control processes in the background of your WordPress blog. WordPress is, after all, a set of web pages hosted on a web server, where nothing happens until it receives a request from the internet—so it requires a trigger.

The trigger comes when a request is received to a serve a special page, called wp-cron-control.php. The script on the page then executes and runs the next job as defined by the schedule.

You can call the page manually by pasting the appropriate URL into a web browser, but this becomes rather impractical when you have a large number of WordPress blogs all requiring the same attention. The solution is to configure what is known as a "cron job" on the server that hosts your WordPress blog. This is a feature that is built in to most hosting accounts, so your hosting company should be able to provide assistance in this area.

W3 Total Cache

W3 Total Cache speeds up the delivery of web pages by caching them in the memory of the server so they can be accessed quickly. The alternative is for the webserver to recreate the page from the content in a database whenever a page is requested, which can slow down the response. Web surfers are fickle, so the last thing you need is your page taking too long to load, as your visitors will give up and go elsewhere.

Yoast SEO

I mentioned earlier that to ensure any post is optimised for search engines, it makes sense to work out the main keywords relating to your post and include them in all the important elements of your post:

• The page title of the post should be in header <h1> tags.

• Subsections should be clearly identified using <h2> and <h3> tags.

• Use bold formatting around some keywords so they stand out.

• Rename images to include your keywords.

• Ensure you populate the description field, including some keywords when adding images.

Fortunately, there are a number of really useful WordPress plugins available that will help you do this. One of the most popular is called "Yoast SEO", it does many things but it's primary function is to help you determine whether you have maximised the use of keywords in a post.

The plugin analyses your posts as you write and provides tips on how to optimise them for your chosen keywords. The plugin is provided free, although there is a premium version that starts at $69 for a single site license. This version unlocks extra features and support should you want to try it.

Yoast also provides video training within the plugin itself that explains how to use it to get the best results.

Google Analytics

This plugin allows you to enter the website's Google Analytics ID so that all the activity on the blog will be tracked. Tracking activity in this manor enables you to gain useful visitor statistics and demographics. You'll find out more about the importance of Google Analytics in the next chapter.

Activate Update Services

Update Services are tools you can use to let other people know you've updated your blog. WordPress will automatically notify popular Update Services that you've updated your blog each time you create or update a post. Unfortunately, this feature gets switched off when Multisite is installed; however, you can reactivate it by installing a plugin called "Activate Update Services" available at the following link:

https://wordpress.org/plugins/activate-update-services/.

Once you have installed and activated the plugin, you will be able to access the Update Services feature from the *Writing Settings* menu option.

By default, only one Update Service is listed, however, there are many others, so to take maximum advantage of this facility, update the box with the following services:

- http://rpc.pingomatic.com
- http://rpc.twingly.com
- http://api.feedster.com/ping
- http://api.moreover.com/RPC2
- http://api.moreover.com/ping
- http://www.blogdigger.com/RPC2
- http://www.blogshares.com/rpc.php
- http://www.blogsnow.com/ping
- http://www.blogstreet.com/xrbin/xmlrpc.cgi
- http://bulkfeeds.net/rpc
- http://www.newsisfree.com/xmlrpctest.php
- http://ping.blo.gs/
- http://ping.feedburner.com
- http://ping.syndic8.com/xmlrpc.php
- http://ping.weblogalot.com/rpc.php
- http://rpc.blogrolling.com/pinger/
- http://rpc.technorati.com/rpc/ping
- http://rpc.weblogs.com/RPC2
- http://www.feedsubmitter.com
- http://blo.gs/ping.php
- http://www.pingerati.net
- http://www.pingmyblog.com
- http://geourl.org/ping
- http://ipings.com
- http://www.weblogalot.com/ping

Minimal Pages

To get your new website off to a good start, I recommend you create the following set of pages and add them to the main menu.

Welcome Page – This will be the main page of the site and will hold your main copy—listing the service(s) available and highlighting the benefits. You may wish to hire a copywriter to help you with this.

Contact Us – This page usually displays the address of the business along with email address, telephone, and fax number. You can also add a form on the page to allow customers to contact you more easily. There are a number of plugins that will allow you to do this. "Contact Form 7" is one of the most popular, and is available via the following link:

https://wordpress.org/plugins/contact-form-7/.

Privacy Policy – Although difficult to prove, many website owners have reported an increase in traffic when they have added a privacy policy. Google seems to like privacy pages in particular. For an example of a privacy page, take a look at http://www.tiledoctor.biz/privacy-policy/

Summary

This chapter detailed the recommended installation configuration for WordPress—taking it from a straightforward blog to a socially connected publishing platform. You will find links to all the recommended plugins and services on the companion website to this book which is detailed in the last chapter "Where to Get More Help".

CHAPTER 7

Essential

Website Tools

Listed in this chapter are a number of tools and services that will work with any website, and best of all—most of them are free.

Google Webmaster Tools

I highly recommend that you sign up for a free Google Webmaster account via the following link.

https://www.google.com/webmasters/tools/

Register your website so you can take advantage of the tools and diagnostic information it makes available. It gives you access to a number of aids that will help you ensure that the site is as Google-friendly as it can be. It will also ensure that your site is included in the Google search index

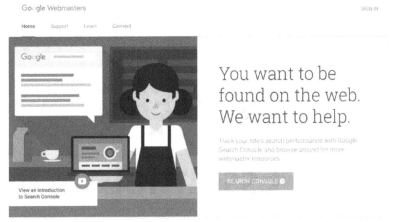

To register your site, you will need to prove you're the owner by uploading a small text file to the root of your web server. Once registered, you can enter the location of your XML sitemap, which will let Google know which web pages to add to its index.

XML sitemaps list all the web pages on your site, and these can then be accessed by search engine bots, which will automatically discover new pages and add them to the search index without any further work being required.

Google is very fast at scanning websites, and once the XML sitemap has been submitted, it won't take long before your pages become indexed and visible in the search engine.

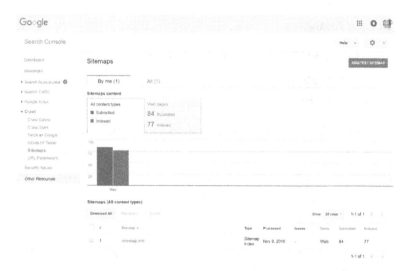

Google's Webmaster tools also provide you with basic search analytics to inform you how your site is performing in the Google index and which keywords are performing best.

The Bing search engine also has similar functionality, and although it doesn't have such a large share of the search market, it's well worth registering to ensure your listed in their index and receive traffic from their users.

http://www.bing.com/toolbox/webmaster

To generate a sitemap, I recommend you install Yoast SEO, which was described in the WordPress plugins section. Alternatively, the Google XML Sitemaps plugin can be installed from:

https://en-gb.wordpress.org/plugins/google-sitemap-generator/

Google Analytics

In order to work out whether all the effort you have put into promoting your site has paid off, you're going to need detailed visitor analytics.

Google's Webmaster tools only provide details collected from the Google search engine itself, so if you looking to collect data about all the visitors to your site from right across the internet, you will need something far more comprehensive.

Like most things related to the internet, Google has a very comprehensive and free tool that you can install for this job—and it's called Google Analytics.

https://analytics.google.com

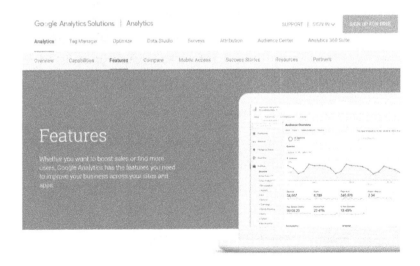

The process is very straightforward and involves creating an account and then registering your website. This in turn will provide you with a tracking ID, which is then added to your website by installing a short script on every web page you wish to track. Adding this script to every page may sound like a lot of work; however, the good news is several plugins you can install for WordPress that will handle this for you, including the following:

https://wordpress.org/plugins/googleanalytics/.

Mailing Lists

Any successful business on the internet relies on its email list to stay in touch and build trust with its customer base. Doing this is vital, and although you can reach out to them via social media channels, having their actual email address is far more valuable as it will allow you to communicate with the customer directly, providing a much greater chance of your message being seen.

 I can't stress enough how essential it is to include the ability to build an email list into your business model.

As well as staying in touch with your existing customers, you can also use mailing lists to capture the email addresses of visitors to promotional sales pages. Normally, the way this works is that you offer something free, such as a report related to your niche, in return for their email address. Once on your list, you can build a relationship with the subscriber, which converts them from a cold to a warm lead. This makes them far more likely to buy the occasional offers you send them.

FREE TIPS

Free Tile, Stone and Grout Maintenance Tips

Name:

Email:

Submit

We respect your email privacy

There are several service providers you can use that will automatically send a series of emails for you which we'll look at on the next page.

For the best results, use a consistent look and feel and send these emails regularly.

Like most things in life, you get what you pay for—and some of these services are very sophisticated indeed.

If you're just starting out with email marketing, then I recommend you take a look at mailchimp.com. Its interface is easy and fun to learn, and it's free until you reach 2,000 subscribers.

Whichever service you choose, it's important to maintain contact with your list by sending them a new email as often as makes sense. Too frequent and many will unsubscribe; too few and they will forget about you. If in doubt about frequency, aim for daily.

www.activecampaign.com	Email marketing, automation, and CRM starts at $9 month.
www.aweber.com	Free for 30 days, then $19 per month.
www.clickfunnels.com	14-day free trial, then $97 per month programs for email subscriptions, product sales, and webinars.
www.constantcontact.com	Free for 60 days, then $20 per month.
www.getresponse.com	Free for 30 days, then $15 per month.
www.infusionsoft.com	$199 month for CRM and marketing automation.
www.mailchimp.com	Free for up to 2,000 subscribers.

Ensuring your emails are read is another matter, and whole books could be written about the science behind which techniques work best. But for now, just follow these simple tips and you won't go far wrong.

1. The first paragraph and email subject should be a single sentence that captures the reader's interest and gives them the essence of the content, which should lure them in.

2. Next, remind the reader why they should read your email, demonstrate your expertise and credibility in this field, and how you got there.

3. Then, add something personal such as an activity or experience you recently had. The reader will feel they're getting to know you, and this helps warm them up so they are more likely to want to read more and buy.

4. Next, provide the content promised, a top tip, a link to more free content, and something educational, entertaining, or inspirational.

5. Add your signature to the bottom of the email, along with a link to your website.

 Remember, first impressions count—so don't be boring.

Google Business and Maps

Google is particularly good at recognising services and place names in search phrases. It generates an interactive map that lists the relevant results as part of the search results on the first page, often leapfrogging the competition by appearing above the organic search results.

What many people aren't aware of is that the results don't come from Google's index of web pages—they come from its business database. To get listed in that database, all you need to do is register with Google Business, which is a free service they provide (http://www.google.co.uk/business/).

Google Business features the ability to upload photographs, add your website, and let your customers leave reviews. Similar to Google+, you can also add posts, all of which generate links that are good for your SEO.

Google reviews are also known to influence the ranking within the Google Business map results, so it's worth encouraging your customers to leave Google reviews. Another factor is known as citations, which refers to the address of the business. The more often that Google can find evidence of your business being listed at the given address, the greater the accuracy implied, and so your ranking within the map results increases.

To maximise citations, it's important to display the business address on the website (ideally in the footer of every page) and register the business in other directories such as Yelp, Foursquare, Hotfrog, Best of the Web, etc.

The following screenshot is that of a typical Google search. Notice how the paid advertising is listed first as expected, then followed by a Google Map showing listings from its business database, with the organic listings at the bottom. The map is highly visual and thus dominates the reader's focus on the page.

dentist new york

All   Maps   Images   Videos   News   More   Settings   Tools

About 15,500,000 results (0.84 seconds)

Dentist New York - MadisonAveSmiles.com
[Ad] www.madisonavesmiles.com/**Dentist** ▼ +1 855-316-0559
Top Notch Dentist in New York! Call for Five Star Express Service
Services: Cosmetic Dentistry, Porcelain Veneers, Sedation Dentistry, Invisible Braces, Dental Implants
Before & After Pictures · Online Appointment
♀ 140 W 58th St a, New York, NY - Open today · 7:00 am – 7:00 pm ▼

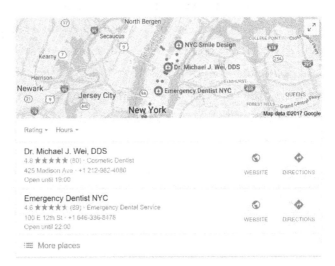

Rating ▾   Hours ▾

Dr. Michael J. Wei, DDS
4.8 ★★★★★ (80) · Cosmetic Dentist
425 Madison Ave · +1 212-982-4080
Open until 19:00

WEBSITE   DIRECTIONS

Emergency Dentist NYC
4.6 ★★★★½ (89) · Emergency Dental Service
100 E 12th St · +1 646-336-8478
Open until 22:00

WEBSITE   DIRECTIONS

⋮☰ More places

Premier Dental Associates of Lower Manhattan
www.premier**dental**associates.com/ ▼
Welcome to Premier Dental Associates of Lower Manhattan! We specialize in ... Call Us: 212-587-0202
| 150 Broadway, Suite 1310, **New York**, NY 10038 ...
Our Team · Patient Info · Location · Referring Doctors

Pearl Dental NYC: Dentist Financial District, New York, NY
www.pearl**dental**nyc.com/ ▼
Trusted **Dentist** serving Financial District, **New York**, NY. Contact us at 212-344-9317 or visit us at 67
Wall Street, Suite 2508, **New York**, NY 10005.
Contact Us · New Patients · Oral Hygiene FAQs · Blog

Summary

Google provides some fantastic free services that are well worth taking advantage of, including Google Business, which is a great way to give local companies a boost in the Google search results. This chapter also discussed building a mailing list, which is another great tool for keeping your current and potential customers warm.

CHAPTER 8

Reputation

Marketing

When looking for a service or product, consumers love to get personal recommendations and it's not uncommon for a typical customer to look at six to ten reviews before making a buying decision. Invariably in the connected world, this happens online and more so when it comes to those under 40 years of age. TripAdvisor is a great example of how the travel industry has been turned upside down by the consumer thirst for more information, as it's now become the most widely recognized, used, and trusted travel website.

It's a proven fact that sales conversions increase as trust increases, so every website selling on the internet needs to convey their reputation in a way that appears to be independent and impartial. Blogging lends itself to that aim quite well, as the more posts a potential customer reads on your site, the more they feel they know and trust you. Adding customer feedback, testimonials, and reviews to the website will help—and for maximum impact, they need to be impartial and come from an independent source.

Most websites have text reviews that rarely change, and to all intents and purposes, may not be impartial or even genuine, so how do viewers know they can trust them? To resolve this problem, there are several independent systems on the market where the reviews are held on an independent website. The added benefit including these is that it also increases the number of backlinks.

Reviews also make great content for a blog or social media post on Twitter.

TileProf @TileDoctorUK Nov 7
Thanks Mr Ashman for your Tile Doctor feedback: 'Arrived promptly and carried out work very professionally and with great care. Happy to rec

Next, you will find three screenshots comparing the textual testimonials you find on most websites to the paid solutions from Reputation.Engineer and Trust Pilot—you can decide which looks more convincing.

Most Websites   Reputation.Engineer   TrustPilot.com

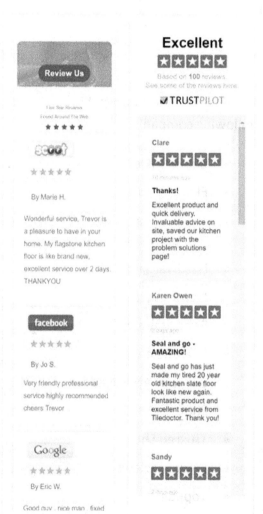

TESTIMONIALS

Had our bathroom tile grout cleaned and protected,pleased with the results.looks as new again...
Nick L, Stoke On Trent

The floor isn't 100 percent pristine, but then it was extremely dirty, had never been sealed, and had been in a bad state for years, so overall we were pleased with how well it came up. Trevor was friendly and helpful, and his positive attitude to taking on the work was our reason for choosing him over a cheaper quote. It looks like a different floor, and for the first time ever since we bought the house (with the floor already in) the room feels clean!
Philip, Melbourne

Trevor certainly improved the look of my bathroom, the tiles now have a lovely shine whereas before they were dull due to a film of grout. Thank you.
Susan, Derby

Trevor was very prompt and sorted my kitchen floor out great.
Karen, Birmingham

Trevor had a very tough job to do getting our Victorian tiles into shape after decades under a Marley tile floor. They were covered in layers of hard glue but Trevor worked exceptionally hard restoring them to like new. Trevor was very friendly and punctual. An excellent job done and we would

Review Us

Five Star Reviews
Found Around The Web
★ ★ ★ ★ ★

★ ★ ★ ★ ☆

By Marie H.

Wonderful service, Trevor is a pleasure to have in your home. My flagstone kitchen floor is like brand new, excellent service over 2 days. THANKYOU

facebook

★ ★ ★ ★ ★

By Jo S.

Very friendly professional service highly recommended cheers Trevor

Google

★ ★ ★ ★ ★

By Eric W.

Good guy , nice man . fixed

Excellent
★ ★ ★ ★ ★
Based on 100 reviews.
See some of the reviews here.
☑ **TRUST**PILOT

Clare
★ ★ ★ ★ ★

Thanks!

Excellent product and quick delivery. Invaluable advice on site, saved our kitchen project with the problem solutions page!

Karen Owen
★ ★ ★ ★ ★

Seal and go - AMAZING!

Seal and go has just made my tired 20 year old kitchen slate floor look like new again. Fantastic product and excellent service from Tiledoctor. Thank you!

Sandy
★ ★ ★ ★ ★

Google has around 30 approved third-party review aggregators who provide them with review data. This data is then included in their search engine listings as a star rating.

Volkswagen Tiguan Review | Auto Express
www.autoexpress.co.uk › Volkswagen ▾
★★★★☆ Rating: 4 - Review by Auto Express
1 Aug 2016 - If your looking for fun you should look elsewhere, but VW's second-generation Tiguan is good at the things that matter in this class.

At the time of producing this book, they include the following companies:

- Bazaarvoice
- Ekomi
- The Feedback Company
- Hardware.info
- Klantenvertellen
- PriceGrabber
- Reviews.co.uk
- Shopper Approved
- ShopAuskunft
- Trusted Shops
- PowerReviews
- Yopi.de
- Zoorate
- Bizrate
- E-Komerco
- Feefo
- KiyOh
- Poulpeo
- Reseller Ratings
- Reevoo
- ShopVote
- TrustedCompany
- Trustpilot
- Verified Reviews
- Yotpo

To get an idea of what these companies offer, we'll have a look at Trustpilot and an alternative system—Reputation.Engineer, which works differently to the other systems.

Trustpilot

Trustpilot was launched in Denmark in 2007 after the founder realised there was nowhere for him to complain about an online purchase his parents had made. Trustpilot has quickly become an industry leader among the international "Reputation" companies and gathers half a million reviews every month.

Its partnership with Google as an approved third-party review aggregator means that review pages for companies registered with Trustpilot show up in Google's index, along with the Trustpilot 5-star rating. However, there is a catch, as Google now insists that a company should have a minimum of 150 reviews in place before they will display the rating.

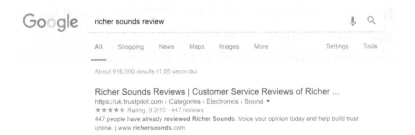

To get your customers on the Trustpilot database, you simply need to send them an email and bcc a specially configured Trustpilot e-mail address (bcc stands for "blind carbon copy" and is standard way of copying another party in on an email without the other recipients knowing). Trustpilot will receive the e-mail and add the customer's email address to its database, and then after a predefined period has elapsed, it will send an email to the customer asking for a review. It's quite a simple system, and has proved to be very effective.

Once you have collected several reviews, you need to showcase the best ones on your website, and you can do this through a widget called a Trustbox. There are a huge array of options available that are easily generated and can be displayed on your website with the addition of a small script.

Reputation.Engineer

The ingenuity of software developers never ceases to impress me, and this latest entrant in the reputation field is revolutionary. Developers realised that consumers have their own favourite and trusted places to leave a review, including Trip Advisor, Google Maps, Yahoo Local, and Facebook to name a few.

Monitoring all of these potential review sites so you can make use of the reviews and respond to criticism is a real headache. But Reputation.Engineer overcomes this by acting as a central hub—actively monitoring the internet, watching for new reviews, and then capturing them in its own database so they can be displayed on your website and syndicated through social media.

Additionally, the software also allows you to create a review form for use on your site so you can capture reviews directly into the database. Cleverly, it can be configured to encourage reviewers leaving good reviews to copy and paste their reviews to other sites such as Facebook, Google, and TripAdvisor, which builds up your reputation across the internet. Negative reviews are redirected to another part of the system where the issues affecting the customer can be investigated and resolved by the business owner.

The feedback form building tool is highly configurable, allowing you to select a format that will blend in with the theme of your site. As well as capturing the feedback, you can set it to collect responses to survey questions. All the information is captured into a CRM, which can be used for future marketing campaigns.

Another great feature that can be set up will automatically publish graphics of the feedback configured with your colours and logo on your social media channels, including Facebook, Twitter, Google+, LinkedIn, Pinterest, Foursquare, and Flickr.

Summary

Having a good reputation online adds social proof and credibility, which you need to be in control of. Disgruntled customers are nosier than happy ones, so directing them to a place where they can vent their issues keeps unhelpful comments out of the public eye.

CHAPTER 9

Outsourcing

The internet has opened up the worldwide employment market, and it has never been easier to take advantage of the lower rates of pay to get work done. If you're implementing an SBN as discussed in this book, then I recommend you take advantage of this and hire someone full time.

I can personally recommend outsourcing to the Philippines, which was under the sovereignty of the United States until 1946. As a result, the majority of people speak fluent English and due to their education system, a large percentage of the population are educated to degree level. Additionally, there is a culture of respect, which makes workers very loyal to their employers and eager to achieve results. With salaries in the region of $300 to $450 a month, depending on skills and experience, it's a perfect place to recruit.

Remember that loyalty is key in outsourcing, as the last thing you need is an outsourcer who runs off and starts a similar business to your own. This is unlikely to happen with workers from the Philippines, as workers there are very risk-averse and are generally not entrepreneurial.

Typical tasks that your outsourcer can do, and that I have hired outsourcers for, include:

- Building followers on Twitter and Pinterest
- Creating adverts on Craigslist
- Creating Facebook pages
- Creating Google accounts
- Creating graphics and videos
- Creating playlists, liking videos, and commenting on videos on YouTube
- Directory registrations
- Posting content and comments on blogs and other sites
- Posting on Google+
- Removing the background from images
- Setting up Google Business accounts
- Setting up WordPress sites including plugins and upgrades
- Tweeting links to posts

I haven't used outsourcers to write copy for blog posts yet, however, you can hire good copywriters from the Philippines. Other skills include AdWords management, Amazon Seller management, customer services, eBay listings, Helpdesk management, programming, web development, and much more.

How to Hire an Outsourcer

For recruitment, you can use an agency; however, it is much more cost-effective to recruitment someone yourself via the following websites:

- http://manila.craigslist.com.ph/
- https://www.onlinejobs.ph/ ($50 per month)

As well as posting jobs, you can also headhunt by viewing online profiles, although you may find that their keen sense of loyalty makes it difficult to recruit someone who is already in post.

Hiring is a straightforward case of reviewing resumes and picking the person with a matching skill set who can provide examples of work they have done previously. If you have to choose between a number of equally talented individuals, then pick the one with the best command of the English language.

Once you have a shortlist of candidates you can conduct interviews over Skype to verify their communication skills and to ensure they have the experience and skills they claim. It also gives them the opportunity to ask you questions and quickly work out any details.

Once you have decided on the right person for you, its worth testing them by setting them a task in line with their advertised skill set. For example, ask them to set up a WordPress site with a specific theme and set of plugins, or if you've hired them for content writing, ask them to research and create the draft of an article. Give them 24 hours to complete the task and see what happens—if they can't complete the task in the time given, then treat this as a red flag.

Assuming all is well and you wish to offer them a job, I recommend you put a contract in place so there are no misunderstandings. The contract should not be one of employment, but rather the hiring of a freelance contractor for their services. This way, there can be no doubt about any entitlement to benefits such as sick pay or a pension etc.

The contractor should then invoice you before they are paid to reinforce the contractor relationship. Ideally, payments would be monthly, but it's not unusual for them to be fortnightly. Remember, you will be transferring funds to another country and this will undoubtedly attract transaction charges, so the less payments you send them, the less fees you will pay. To transfer funds take a look at www.orbitremit.com who operate worldwide.

Here are some other tips you need to be are of when hiring
someone from the Philippines:

- It's normal to pay a bonus equivalent to a month's salary at Christmas.
- There are a lot of national holidays in the Philippines, which you need to consider; see www.portalseven.com/calendar/ for more details.
- Remember, the Philippines is a third-world country and internet speeds are much slower than in the west.
- Tropical storms are known to knock out power and connections from time to time, so don't be surprised if they occasionally disappear for a few days.
- Filipinos are very family-orientated and may need time off for family occasions.
- Filipinos are very respectful, so don't be surprised if they call you Sir or Madam all the time.

Managing Outsourcers

The way you manage your outsourcer depends on you, and you may find yourself micromanaging initially until you get a good feel for how they work. Personally, I set tasks for each outsourcer for each day via email and ask them to reply and confirm that each individual task has been completed. I usually set these up as draft emails in advance so they are ready to go.

One recommendation from many people is that it's critical to get an email from the outsourcer every day outlining the tasks they have completed, any problems they had, and how they worked around them. This email should be a condition of payment for a day's work.

Here are some tips to build trust and get the best from your outsourcer:

- Be prepared to spend time teaching them how to do things, even though it's probably quicker initially to do it yourself.
- Send encouraging/constructive comments when they do good work.
- Use a screen capture tool such as Jing to send short video messages/instructions as this helps them to get to know you.
- Never threaten to fire them, as this is very negative for any worker. If their work isn't up to scratch, make sure they are aware and give them chance to turn things around. Naturally, if things don't change, you will need to let them go.
- Always pay them promptly.
- Pay occasional bonuses for doing exemplary work.

Content Writers

The following are a number of online services that specialise in the creation of articles; prices range from as little as $4 per article up to $300.

- www.digital-gladiators.com

- www.pbnbutler.com

- www.peopleperhour.com

- www.verycopy.Com

- www.wordagents.com

When contacting writers, make sure you specify that you want them to write search engine friendly articles and inform them of your target keywords.

Gig Work

As an alternative to hiring a full-time outsourcer, consider hiring people to complete one-off jobs or "gigs" as they are often called. The following sites are great for finding quality people at low rates:

- www.fiverr.com

- www.gigbucks.com

- www.seoclerks.com

- www.tenbux.com

When using services such as Fiverr, look out for the following:

- Check their reviews; a good seller will have long reviews and repeat buyers.

- Monitor their response time when you contact them— someone who responds very quickly may indicate they are not particularly busy and for good reason; conversely, you don't want someone who takes days to get back to you.

- Review their profile and see what other gigs they offer. Ideally, you want to hire an expert rather than a jack of all trades.

I highly recommend Fiverr, which I've used on many occasions to buy Facebook page likes and Twitter followers. Incidentally, this is something I highly recommend you do as no one likes to be the first person to like a Facebook page or be the first follower.

Summary

Getting your websites to the top of the natural Google search listings takes a lot of work setting up accounts, configuring, writing, and posting content—all of which is repetitive and labour-intensive. Given the low cost of labour in the Philippines and other countries, it makes sense to recruit someone to do the work for you rather than doing it yourself. As the saying goes, "Better to work on your business rather than in your business".

Chapter 10

Next Steps

Regardless of the size of your business, there is no reason why you can't take advantage of the strategies suggested in this book—it's just a question of scaling them to meet your needs and keeping up the momentum by putting a system in place to generate and publicise your content on a regular basis.

With this in mind, I've put together some steps you can use as a checklist to get your own business on track.

Step 1 – Set up a Google Account

It's well worth setting up a new account on Google from the outset, which you can use as a central point from which to manage all your activities and registrations, separate from anything else. Additionally, having a separate account from your own will also enable you to easily share access with your outsourcer or employee.

Step 2 – Discover Your Keywords

Knowing which keywords to target is the foundation to designing your solution. You may wish to revisit the chapter on keywords at this point.

Step 3 - Design Your Solution

The design and scale of the SBN solution basically boils down to how much content you are likely to be able to generate. After all, there's little point setting up a blog if you don't have anything to publish on it. This may require some brainstorming and inventive, "out of the box" thinking to flesh out; use your keyword list from Step 2 as inspiration here.

Reorder your keyword list into obvious groups, one of which should form your primary source of stories for your main blog, while everything else will form your second series of blogs. With Tile Doctor, this was always a simple decision as each territory had its own blog, while the types of tile being worked on formed the second series of blogs.

Step 4 - Creation

Once you have decided on the structure, you need to give some thought to domain names, as you will need to register a minimum of two. At this point, you may wish to review the Google Search algorithm section in chapter 1, which contains more recommendations on choosing a domain name and hosting company.

Once your domain names have been registered, you will need to install WordPress configured in Multisite mode with your chosen theme, minimal pages, and the recommended plugins (see the chapter 6 on WordPress for details).

Remember, if you have hired an outsourcer, most of the tasks in this section can be given to them to complete.

At this point, it's a good ideal to register the site with Google's and Bing's Webmaster Tools (see chapter 7 on Essential Website Tools). This will ensure that the site and its posts appears in their index, and they also provide some valuable statistics later on. You can use the Google account you set up earlier for this.

Step 5 – Set Up Social Media Accounts

Before posting anything on your blog, it makes sense to ensure that anything you do post will be distributed as much as possible on social media, so take the time to set up the accounts now. If you're using the Social Link Machine plugin, configure it with the new account details.

To save time, at this stage you may wish to focus on the top platforms such as Facebook, Google+, Twitter, and Pinterest, then add the rest later.

Step 6 - Start Posting Content

You have now configured your publishing platforms, so you're ready to start posting content. Ideally, you should aim to post at least one 500-word story per day, which may sound like a challenge, but once you get a system worked out to generate content, you will find this becomes much easier. A calendar may prove useful at this point in order to send you reminder about key dates and activities etc. Google Calendar works well for this, and you can use the Google account you created at the start of this section to send you reminders. Write your posts with your keywords in mind and use the Yoast SEO plugin to keep it optimised.

Once posted on your primary blog and syndicated through its social media channels, you then re-post it on your secondary blog with a link at the bottom back to the original post. Remember, the anchor text of the link should contain the keywords relevant to the post. Once posted, syndicate the new post via your social media channels. Of course, if you have set up the Social Link Machine plugin, this will be done automatically for you.

Daily Routine

Once you have everything configured and your first post is live, you need to get into a regular routine for posting content. The routine I set up for Tile Doctor works as follows:

Step 1: Copywriter receives new content from Tile Doctor, renames the images to include keywords, and reviews the text to add headers, background information, and relevant links. They format this into a story ready for posting. Copy and images are copied into a shared folder on Dropbox.

Step 2: The outsourcer now takes over the remaining tasks and downloads the new story from Dropbox. They post the copy along with images on to the related Tile Doctor blog, add keywords as tags, and add a comment.

Step 3: The best pair of before and after images are added to the main page of the blog and a new image is created and posted to Twitter (with #hashtags) and Pinterest.

Step 4: If sufficient images are supplied with the post, then a video is created along with relevant titles and uploaded to YouTube. The video is also added to the main page of the Tile Doctor blog.

Step 5: The post is reposted on to the related authority site along with relevant tags, a comment, and a link back to the original blog post.

Step 6: The best pair of before and after images are added to the main page of the blog.

Step 7: The before and after image is used as part of a second tweet directed to a different relevant Twitter user account with a link back to the blog post.

Step 8: The post is reposted on another related blog if relevant.

Whilst all of this is going on, Social Link Machine is working quietly in the background, adding the post to social media accounts and generating links.

One Last Thing

Once your SBN is running and you have a system in place to generate content, pay regular visits to your Webmaster and Analytics accounts. These accounts enable you to see which keywords are responding best, so you can make decisions about where to better focus or reduce your Google AdWords budget.

You should also look for opportunities to grow your network by adding new blogs and social media accounts where you can repost and syndicate your content.

Where to Get More Help

The internet is a fast-moving, rapidly-changing environment, so it's highly likely that the website links detailed in this book will at some point in the future no longer work. With this in mind, we have created a website where you will find a companion guide to the book:

http://www.socialblog.network/.

On this site, you will find the latest updates, strategies, links to plugins and other recommendations. You will also find details of the many services we offer all designed around the implementation of an SBN, including Multisite hosting, configuration, reputation marketing, content generation, and training workshops.

GLOSSARY

Anchor Text – The visible text in a link to another web page.

API – Application Program Interface, allows computer programs to talk to each other through a well-defined interface.

Authority Site – A website recognised by Google as an authority in a specific niche.

BCC – Blind Carbon Copy, a standard e-mail function that allows you to add one or more recipients to an email without the other recipients being made aware.

Encryption – The data that flows between a web browser and server is sent as text by default, which can with the right tools be intercepted. Encryption scrambles the text to make it unreadable without the right key.

Going Viral – This is when your content is so popular it continues to be voluntarily shared across the internet, allowing it to reach thousands of people in a short period of time.

Google Algorithm – The process by which Google determines how to order website pages for a given search phrase.

HTML – **Hyper Text Markup Language, the language used to** describe a web page over the internet.

Latency – The time taken between making a web page request and receiving the response.

Link Juice – Envisages the flow of links to a web page.

Low Hanging Fruit – Something that is easy to achieve.

Metatags – Hidden HTML statements used to categorise and describe the contents on a web page.

Paid Search – Refers to the use of services such as Google Adwords and Bing Ads to get to the top of the search engine listings.

PBN – Private Blog Network, a group of blogs with the same owner used to generate backlinks.

SBN – A PBN that has been enhanced to syndicate content to social media.

RSS – Really Simple Syndication, a standard used for the distribution of headlines and sometimes content to a wide readership.

SEO – Search Engine Optimisation, a process used by web developers to improve the ranking of a website in a search engine such as Google and Bing.

SSL – Secure Socket Layer, a form of technology used to encrypt internet traffic between sender and receiver.

Syndicated – A term made popular by the newspaper industry to define the controlled distribution of news articles.

Widgets – Small scripts in WordPress that provide a specific function and can be easily added into the sidebar of a site.

XML Sitemap – A file in a standard format that lists the web pages on a site that can be read by Google and other search engines about the organisation of your site's content.

Vlog – A video blog, as made popular by YouTube, which allows its users to group videos into channels.

Vlogger – Someone who regularly publishes videos to their channel on YouTube or similar service.